Born in the Delta

Born in the Delta

Reflections on the Making of a
Southern White Sensibility

Margaret Jones Bolsterli

The University of Arkansas Press
Fayetteville
2000

Originally published by The University of Tennessee Press, 1991

13 12 11 10 09   6 5 4 3 2

Delta landscape. Photo by the author.

Material in the chapters "The Delta" and "The Table" appeared previously in the *Arkansas Times*. It is used here by permission.

"The Delta" appeared previously in the *Southern Humanities Review* under the title "The Very Food We Eat." It is used here by permission.

Designer: Kay Jursik

♾ The paper used in this publication meets the minimum requirements of the American National Standard for Permanence of Paper for Printed Library Materials Z39.48-1984.

Library of Congress Cataloging-in-Publication Data

Bolsterli, Margaret Jones.
    Born in the delta : reflections on the making of a Southern white sensibility / Margaret Jones Bolsterli.
        p. cm.
    Originally published : Knoxville : University of Tennessee Press, 1991.
    ISBN 1-55728-616-7 (pbk. : alk. paper)
    1. Desha County (Ark.)—Social life and customs. 2. Plantation life—Arkansas—Desha County. 3. Southern States—Civilization. 4. Bolsterli, Margaret Jones—Childhood and youth. 5. Desha County (Ark.)—Biography. I. Title.

F417.D4 B65 2000
976.7'85—dc21

                                                                    00-041759

"Tell about the South. What's it like there. What do they do there. Why do they live there. Why do they live at all."

Harvard students to Quentin Compson

"Now I want you to tell me just one thing more. Why do you hate the South?"

Shreve to Quentin

"I dont hate it," Quentin said, quickly, at once, imme-diately; "I dont hate it," he said. *I dont hate it* he thought, panting in the cold air, the iron New England dark: *I dont. I dont! I dont hate it! I dont hate it!*

William Faulkner, *Absalom, Absalom!*

For Olivia Sordo

Contents

Acknowledgments xiii

The Delta 1

The Household 21

Talk 47

Violence 53

White and Black 65

Friends and Neighbors 79

Moderate Brimstone 89

Books and Learning 97

The Table 109

The Afterglow of the Confederacy 123

Illustrations

Map of Desha County, Arkansas   2
Margaret Jones Bolsterli at seventeen   22
The Jones Family in 1901   22
Aunt Sally posing with Uncle Luther's rifle, about 1898   23
Zena Cason Jones and Margaret in 1932   23
The Jones family in 1932   24
Pauline Jones Lloyd and a school friend in 1934   24
The author in 1985   24
Hunting camp, about 1898   54
The Cheshire family at nearby Red Fork, about 1896   80

Acknowledgments

This book was a long time in the writing and has a varied provenance. In the first place, it stems from a series of conversations about the South and my childhood in it that I held with the late poet and novelist John Clellon Holmes and his wife Shirley, a fellow southerner, over a period of ten years. John encouraged me to write what I told, and I did take notes. Then, when *Roots* was playing on the television, my brother Bob came by full of enthusiasm and asked rather pointedly why nobody had done the same thing for "us." Meanwhile, I was working on a massive study of the effect of the black presence in the South on the southern white consciousness, when it occurred to me that, without a certain perspective, many readers would not know how the southern consciousness differed from others. Since I thought I had that perspective, I started an outline. Then, finally, one afternoon my sister Pauline and I were driving over to the museum at Arkansas Post for some research I was doing on a family from that neighborhood. She turned to me and said, "Why don't you write about your own family?" So I did.

Many people read the manuscript over the years and offered advice and encouragement. It is one of the great regrets of my life that I did not get the work finished in time for John and Shirley Holmes to see it. However, I am confident that no-one would have understood the reasons better. Willard B. Gatewood, Jr., and Elizabeth Payne of the History Department, University of Arkansas; Sidney Burris, Brian Wilkie, and Debora Shuger of the English Department, University of Arkansas; and James C. Cowan of the English Department, University of North Carolina, Chapel Hill, gave me the encouragement that I needed to finish the project. I am grateful to all.

I wish my family pleasure in the shared memories they will find here, and I beg their indulgence for the interpretations, which are entirely mine.

Born in the Delta

1

The Delta

I was born in the delta region of Arkansas, in Desha County, near the point where the Arkansas runs into the Mississippi. But *Delta*, in this case, means more than topography. It is also a landscape of the mind, formed by the culture that blossomed out of that rich soil as surely as the cotton on which that culture was based, and this landscape of the mind defines people as certainly as do individual Swiss cantons or French provinces or English counties. When I first went north, I was surprised to learn that there were people in the world who did not know that Arkansas has both a delta and a culture that goes with southern lowlands. Several years later, crossing the German border into Switzerland in a meadow where I had expected a wall of Alps to begin, I was able to place their ignorance in perspective. Most people who think about Arkansas at all think only of mountains and hillbillies. But the fact is that my section of the state, roughly the eastern third, is part of the great level Mississippi floodplain, where centuries of flooding have laid down layer upon layer of the richest topsoil imaginable. It is such perfect soil for raising cotton that people considered it worth the risk long before flood control was possible. The frontier came late, stayed a long time, and when it moved on, left a southern culture. For when people started moving there in the early nineteenth century, it was not to start a new life so much as to find a place where the old ways could flourish. Cotton, along with the social system it took to make it profitable, grew like a weed, and if it proved impossible for settlers to duplicate in the remote backwoods the particular style of civilized

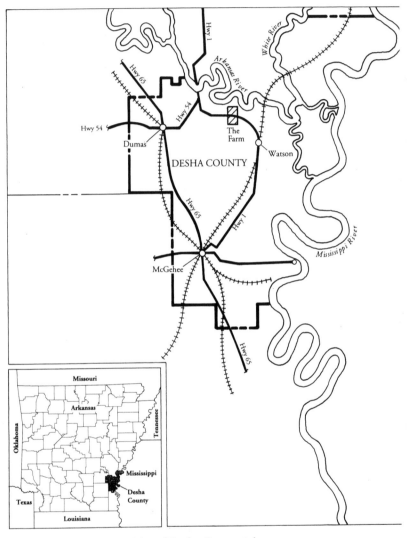

Map of Desha County, Arkansas.

life they had left in Kentucky, Virginia, or even Mississippi, it was not for lack of trying. The ideal was certainly there. The Delta nurtured southern traditions that people who went further west had a harder time retaining. Thus, while in Northwest Arkansas there was such ambivalence about the Civil War that brothers might find themselves in opposing armies, Southeast Arkansas, the heart of the Delta, was as secessionist as Georgia.

Growing up there forged in me a sensibility that I share with thousands of other southerners – a way of feeling, of seeing, that is different not only from the sensibility of people who come from mountains, but also from that of those who come from anywhere else in the world. We are different from others because of the place we came from. Sorting out the reasons why this is so has been an occasional preoccupation with me for more than thirty years. If this introspection seems self-indulgent, it must be remembered that people from the Lower South are frequently reminded by others of some of our more obvious differences, such as patterns of speech, even our tone of voice, a taste for certain foods, the habit of seeing the world as material to be rearranged into stories. But these are only the *outer* signs of inner differences so deep that outlanders cannot possibly see them. Furthermore, we have but to open our mouths, not only to be reminded of our differences, but also to be accused of the hereditary guilt that festers in most of us like an old war wound and which in many of our best writers has been the grain of sand that worried itself into a pearl. Where else in America has the guilt associated with racism led to a characteristic body of literature, a literature of conscience? This brand of guilt, which has gnawed like a serpent in the bosom of such diverse writers as William Faulkner, Lillian Smith, and Walker Percy, is not the stock in trade of their northern, western, or eastern contemporaries. The conception of Yoknapatawpha County and its people would have been impossible to John Steinbeck, Ernest Hemingway, Norman Mailer, or Saul Bellow, yet it is such familiar territory to southerners that they tend to give Faulkner more credit for organization than invention.

Not all the South is Delta; all southerners are not alike. There are many "Souths," but there is something common to all of them not found in other regions of this country, and southerners tend to think of themselves as having been shaped by "place." For example, the sub-title of Harry Crews' stunning autobiography *A Childhood* is "The Biography of a Place," and the autobiographical essays in *Killers of the Dream* are Lillian Smith's attempt to explain how the "South could override all other influences, including deep religious faith, to teach people how to be 'white.'" It is the uniqueness of the place that makes us what we are, as a line in a poem by James T. Whitehead goes, "We come from where we get the wound." V.S. Naipaul says in his recent travel book *A Turn in the South* that it is a distinctive mark of southern identity that we feel that a fabric of community exists for us to claim a thread in. What I write here is an attempt to trace the intricate patterns in my own particular piece of the tapestry.

The salient *fact* is that I grew up on what some might call a small cotton plantation down there in the 1930s, and the combination of nature and the particular brand of civilization represented by that farm in that place and time gave me a turn of mind that can only be explained by explaining the context. The only way I see how to do this without resorting to a construct like fiction is to reflect on the bits and pieces of my memory. So, rather than reshape the past into a sequential narrative that would have to be fiction to be read-able, I have decided to let that sensibility reveal itself episodically – to tell, in a somewhat circular fashion and in light of what I have thought about it over the years, what I remember. For, as I did not know how flat the land there was until I left and saw hills to compare it with, neither did I know that I had a "southern" sensibility until I came up against the rest of the world.

The sky in the Delta is as big as the sky in Montana, but the over-whelming impression is of the flatness of the land. It is absolutely level, and the flow of vision is broken only by trees in the distance; there is always a blue haze around the feet of those trees, so the hori-zon, year round, has layers of color. The trees still left are usually on bayous or brakes, since most of the woods have been cleared to make more and more fields. In 1936, when I started school, there were still long stretches of once-cut-over woods between our house and the school six miles away at Watson. My father told of his childhood, when the woods were thousands of acres of live-oak trees, notable for their lack of underbrush. He said it was like riding through a vast forest of umbrellas, and you could see a deer for a long, long way. He thought that the first cutting of those trees for lumber and then the 1927 Flood had brought the undergrowth that caused so much trouble to a hunter. The only oaks on our place now, left from that first cut of timber, are in the graveyard, where four generations of my family are buried and where I have picked my spot. Now the fields are bigger than ever. The standard length of a row is a quarter of a mile; some are longer. The fields take on different patterns and colors with the seasons, but the striking impression of vastness never leaves. The transitions are like a great graphic display that changes and flows but does not alter the screen itself.

After flatness, the second impact is of lushness, more like an over-ripe pear than anything else I can think of. In summer everything is a green that threatens to grow over you if you stand still to look at it. Everything is sprouting, growing, dying of completion, to be reborn and start the whole cycle over again. The soil itself, in a layer eighteen feet deep, is rich sandy loam or a particular kind of clay called buckshot or gumbo because, when it is wet, it is as sticky as gumbo, but it dries in granules the size of buckshot. The richness of this soil is legendary; they claim that if you stick a broomstick in the ground it will grow.

For over fifty years, until I bought a farm of my own in the mountain country of Northwest Arkansas, I think that farm in the Delta was the only place in the world that I took seriously. Certainly I have left every other place without a backward glance or a moment's nostalgia. The landscape of our farm was so much the landscape of my mind that it became the touchstone of what the earth, in particular instances, should look like. I found myself comparing every-

thing to it. Once, on the drive from Moscow to its airport, I realized
that I was staring at a pasture that would have looked exactly like
ours if only there had been a Coca-Cola sign in one corner of it,
lending shade to a few white-faced cows. Another time, I woke in
the middle of the night on a train going from Copenhagen to Inns-
bruck and raised the shade to look out on a moonlit German field
that could have passed for one of ours if it had been covered with
dried cotton stalks instead of wheat stubble. Corot's paintings always
remind me of trees on the horizon in the Delta, especially the ones
you can see from the front porch at the farm. Perhaps that is what
it means to say that travel is broadening; it gives you new ways of
seeing what you knew to start with. But one thing is certain; this
place would not mean what it does to me without the stories and
associations that go with it. For the place is so firmly situated in
what might be called my "mindscape" that the two are inseparable.
One is as permanent as the other, and while the culture had its roots
in the evil and shame of slavery and racism, this heritage its heirs,
at the time I am telling about, were powerless to change. The caste
system was as complex and rigid as that of medieval Europe, and
white landowners were at the top of the hierarchy. Little wonder that
so much significance was attached to the land.

Although our place was no larger than a wheat farm in Kansas
or a corn farm in Iowa, the different way in which it was operated
gave it the characteristics of a plantation and all the problems that
go with that particular method of farming. The basis of the plantation economy at the time I am describing was indebtedness. The
landowner borrowed enough money from a bank to make a crop
and then lent it to his sharecroppers, most of whom were black,
against half of the proceeds. He furnished seed, tools, animals to pull
the plows, and guarantee of enough money to clothe, feed, and provide medical care for the sharecropper's family until harvest, when
the tenant would be obliged to give the landowner half the crop and
then, out of his own half, pay back the money he had "drawn" for
his and his family's expenses. The owner then would repay the bank

for his "furnish" loan. If no money was made, the chain of indebtedness was carried over to the next year. It was a matter of principle
with my family not to mortgage the land for furnish money. This
was considered the way to certain ruin. Instead, every mule and
piece of equipment on the place was listed as collateral, including
worn-out combines and cultivators and hay balers that had not
worked in years. The responsibility my father had for lending his
money carefully, because he would be called upon in his turn to pay
it back to the bank, led to extreme parsimony when it came to letting
the tenants have what they asked for. I remember particularly long
discussions he had with a tenant named Arthur Thomas, who had
a large family, always made money for us, and consequently had a
lot of requests that he, quite reasonably, thought should be listened
to, but that my father met with almost pathological skepticism. The
size of a tenant's family was extremely important, because the more
members in it, the more land they could work. A man with a hardworking wife and eight or ten children could pick a bale of cotton
a day, roughly 1,300 pounds before ginning. And, in addition to
crops made on shares with these tenants, landowners almost always
had a "day crop," to be worked by laborers paid by the day – usually
tenants on the place. If a sharecropper did not have enough workers
in his family to get his cotton chopped and picked, others were sent
in to help, and he would be required to help pay for this out of his
half of the proceeds. It was a brutal, unforgiving system that gave
the landowner, literally, the power of life and death. I have never
heard anybody actually engaged in it defend it as a method of farming, but we inherited it along with the land, and it was the only
system my father understood. When he died in 1957, my brother
mechanized the place so thoroughly that three or four salaried tractor drivers and machine operators could do the work that it had
taken sixty or seventy people of various sizes to do in 1937. Mechan-
ization like this displaced people who had no skill at anything but
farmwork and drove them off the land into the ghettos of Detroit
and Chicago. Cruel payment for generations of backbreaking labor.

The displacement of tenants by machines came later to our farm than to many, because my old-fashioned father so adamantly opposed it. He did not understand how machines that were so expensive could ever profitably replace mules and people. By the time he died, the old system of farming had been in process of disintegration for so long that the migration of southern tenant farmers to urban areas in other parts of the country had become a tidal wave before the last of our sharecroppers and renters joined it. As the historians Pete Daniel and Jack T. Kirby have demonstrated, the displacement of southern tenant farmers by machinery was only one part of a pattern of change begun during the Great Depression. The trend was encouraged by government subsidy of crop allotment that took land out of cultivation and by the fear that laborers who had left the farms for factories during World War II never again would be available for hand work in the fields. But the cold facts on the page do not hint at the human misery behind them. A young man who remained on our place as a tractor driver told of visiting his relatives in a high-rise building in Chicago, where they lived on the fifth floor and were terrified to take the elevator because they were afraid of who else might get on it with them. They walked up and down, although the lights were always broken out on the stairways. He told of climbing the four flights in pitch dark, with one hand on the wall for guidance and a loaded pistol in the other.

I have said that it was not size but method that made our place more like a plantation than a farm; another difference in management, besides sharecropping, lay in the fact that the women's sphere was so separate from the men's. Women of the landowning class did not work in the fields nor cook gigantic dinners for hired hands during harvest, as they would have done on such a farm in the Middle West, or perhaps even in northwestern Arkansas. This is one of the points where the Delta as topography and the Delta as mindscape intersect. For the culture that went with the plantation system gave the practice of patriarchy in the South a distinctive flavor that it lacked in other parts of America. One suspects that the place of a woman in the Deep South was where it was – on the highest pedestal her men could afford – because plantation culture, to which everyone white aspired, dictated that certain work was degrading for white women and, more to the point, that if they had to do it, the men who were supposed to be able to protect them from it were more dishonored than they. Furthermore, it was felt that white women had to be protected from black men. The effect of this protection was to isolate them in what were, metaphorically speaking, harems that included all of a man's women. His mother, girlfriend, sisters, wife, and daughters, if not indeed all "decent" women, were to be given his protection if they in turn would "behave," thereby protecting his name and ideals. The pedestal had to be highest where the concentration of blacks was heaviest, which probably explains why the situation seemed so extreme in the Delta. The need for this protection made it imperative that southern women be well-trained in the skills necessary to secure a husband, and, since a man's worth would be compromised by a wife who worked, it follows that the most valuable wives of all were the most useless. So the strengths that would have brought success in the marketplace or professions were not encouraged. Good marks in school and the ability to play the piano were expected of girls as accomplishments that would make them good wives and mothers, not as preparation for careers. As for learning to run a farm, what greater waste of time could have been imagined for someone who never would be allowed to do it unless all the men in her family dropped dead? It would have seemed ridiculous, if not downright scandalous, for me to take a university degree in agriculture, as two of my brothers did, who were not going to be farmers either. This "cult of belledom" differed from station to station in the social hierarchy only in degree, not in kind. To this day, the ideal for southern women is still so influenced by nostalgia for the "southern belle" that when I poll my women students for names of women in fiction who, at some time in their lives, they would have liked to be, the lists almost invariably include Scarlett O'Hara as well as Nancy Drew. Shirley Abbott, in *Womenfolk*, her account of growing up in western Arkansas, remarks that this aspiration toward belledom was one of the noticeable differences between southern and western women in her freshman class at Texas State College for Women in the 1960s. If the influence of belledom reached all the way to circumstances such as hers, among dirt farmers in the mountains near Hot Springs, no wonder that it was strong where I was, with my feet literally on the soil that had nurtured such dreams in the first place. The training for womanhood that the culture demanded was about as subtle as a sledgehammer and equally effective, whether one resisted it or not.

If our four hundred acres had been in Iowa, a strapping tomboy like me would have driven a tractor or, at least, have fed the stock. But in our world, to have his daughter doing such work would have spelled disgrace for my father, who would have locked me up to starve before he let me go to the fields. My brothers could drive tractors and feed stock; I could have died respectably from sunstroke while working a flowerbed, but I could not chop cotton. This position was so extreme that, when my brothers had all gone off to World War II and the place was rented out so we no longer had a barn full of animals, Daddy paid a man to feed my horse, his horse, and the two mules that he kept because he could not bear to be without livestock. All I would have had to do to feed those animals was tilt corn down from the barn loft into their trough; I was frequently there anyway at feeding time, putting up my horse. Yet my father's pride depended on my not pulling the handle on the trap door of the corn bin.

The spheres of influence of men and women were separate indeed, yet women had an awesome power over men which they exercised by quiet, cunning manipulation. My mother *never* made a direct request for anything or any course of action, nor did she ever, in word, in deed, or probably even in thought, belittle my father or allude to his shortcomings. But she might say something like "Wouldn't it be nice if we had a deeper well . . ." Daddy would meet such sallies either with silence or logical resistance, but one day, exactly as if he had thought it up himself, it would be part of his plans to have a deep well so that our water would be soft. It might take years for such seeds to sprout, but patience was considered one of such a woman's virtues. Her hints could concern anything from major decisions about the crops to whether the orchard could be mowed before the preacher came to dinner on Sunday. As long as they were only *suggestions*, her ideas could be entertained. By the same token, my father never criticized the household and yard operations, since her authority in this sphere was as absolute as his in the fields and barns. Her actual manipulation was extended to include my brothers, and the training in ways to exercise this skill was extended to me. My inclination was to meet my father head on, tell him what I wanted to do, and then negotiate a compromise through heated discussion. Mother would wring her hands in despair and say to me, "If you would just learn how to *handle* your father, you could get him to do anything in the world you want him to." But when I was fourteen, the impatience of youth was whispering in the other ear that I would be too old to care by the time Daddy got used to the idea that it was all right for me to drive alone the twelve miles to Dumas, the town where I went to high school. (In those days, in the rural South you could do pretty much what you were big enough to do, so I had my first driver's license at thirteen.) My father was a king in our house, but just as surely, my mother was a queen and treated as such. In other parts of the country, I have come to see the difference between that order of things and households where the man is king and the woman frequently is considered a servant. The organization of patriarchy was simply different in the South.

In spite of the method our place shared with plantation operations much larger in size, it would have been pretentious to call ours a *plantation*, and we were too secure in the position we held to need pretensions. Perhaps the most comforting thing about a stratified caste system is the certainty of knowing your place on the ladder. Our place was a farm. The very word *plantation* conjures up visions of white columns and a social life a pitch or two above ours. There were several plantations like that around, and it is a mark of what we did share that two of my best friends in high school were daughters of an incredibly wealthy planter family. What we shared with these people who farmed fourteen thousand acres, compared with our four hundred, was simple to state and almost too complex to describe: we were not *common.*

Common, in those days, was a social and moral term used by southerners to maintain the system. The theory held that the concept *common* was a delicate and precise instrument with which to measure every aspect of behavior. The opposite of *common* was *nice.* As mother cats teach their kittens to hunt and wash their faces after meals, our mother taught us how not to be common.

"Don't chew with your mouth open, it's common."

"When offering refreshments, never say, 'Do you want a Coke?' Instead, say 'Would you like a Coca Cola? Or, 'Would you care for a Coca Cola?'

"Never say, 'I enjoyed myself.' Say, rather, 'I enjoyed the evening very much.'" (It is common to enjoy yourself and not the company of others.)

Common people draw attention to themselves; they have loud voices, wear loud colors, admit to having feelings, and do not know any better than to mention bodily functions. Common women let their slips show and their stocking seams remain crooked and, given a choice, would have two cheap sweaters instead of one good one. Common people of either sex might use profanity. Nice women would not. Ever. Nice men might swear among other men, but never around nice women and girls. I do not recall ever hearing mentioned what they did around common women. Common people were the ones who got drunk and swore and stole and murdered and went to jail. The daughters of common people were welcome to come to our house if I invited them, but I could not go to theirs. When I made a new friend, I would wait cringing for Mother's quiet assessment. I did not want it to matter and would swear that it would not, but when she murmured "common" about the family of a new acquaintance, it affected me. The friendship could never be what I was always looking for, a partnership between equals. I could never spend the night at my new friend's house, and knowing that Mother felt the way she did, I could never see her with unbiased eyes. I hated it with every fibre in my soul, but I could not ignore it. Northerners seem to think that, in the South, *white trash* is a term used frequently for people on the lowest rung of the social ladder. The rung was certainly there and the term was understood to define it, but in my house it would have been considered common to use the words *white trash. Common* was the worst you could say without sounding common yourself. You could be dirt poor and landless and still not be common, while common people could get hold of both land and money. It was thought that once they did, however, with a great deal of additional effort, they might eventually transcend their condition and not be common anymore. This may be amusing now that the world has become egalitarian; as an older southerner recently remarked to me, "Honey, *everybody's* common now." But it was serious then; it was the glue that held the social ladder together.

The connection between the concept "common" and money was complex and tenuous. Not being common implied having manners, and having manners frequently, but not always, implied that a family had had leisure at some time or other. Those who were poor but not common might, then, have descended from people who at some time had had more in the way of financial ease than the family had at present. People who lived in houses on the point of collapse, but who at some time had been associated with well-kept ones, were acceptable in any circumstances. On the other hand, common people with new money, new houses, and new cars would be categorized as such until the day they died. "Poor little thing," Mother would say about the unfortunate child of such a family, who might have disgraced herself by something like accepting a compliment without saying thank-you, "How could she be expected to know any better?" And when Mother said, "Don't forget that you have had *advantages*," she did not mean that we had money. The term for that was *oppor-*

tunities. What she meant was that we had been taught how to behave, a skill more valuable than money because it would allow us to travel freely in any society where, in fact, there would be *opportunities*. It seemed to take about a generation for monied but common people to lose the tag, and it was a matter of their changing their behavior to accord with their rising aspirations, rather than of people's coming to tolerate their ways because they had money.

Terms for the training required for such manners were "raising" and "having background." One day my father came home from Baxter Gladden's store, where he loved to visit a few hours every day during the slack farming season, with the following tale that delighted him. He and several other white men were sitting around the stove when a small black boy came in with a nickel, bought a Hershey bar, carefully unwrapped half of it without touching the chocolate, then turned to my father, held out the candy bar and said, "Mr. Jones, would you care for a piece?" The boy offered it to each man in turn, and each gravely but politely declined. "Now, *that* child," Daddy said, glaring at me, "had raising." The term "common" was applied to blacks as well as whites, by both blacks and whites. One would not have a common black woman working in the house because, after all, the white children would come under her influence. And Victoria Figures, who worked for us, would lift her eyes from the ironing board, gaze off into space and deliver her final word on some black woman she didn't approve of: "Why, she's as common as dishwater."

Our emotional attachment to the land was absolute. When I was a child, my heart would come into my throat when Bob, the brother five years older than I, who knew exactly how to worry me, would say that if we did not have a good crop we might lose the place. It had already on two occasions been "up" for back taxes, and somebody had stepped in and saved it for the sake of the family. Uncle Gordon and Aunt Maggie had let the parcels they inherited slip through their fingers and were held up as examples of what happens to people who "live beyond their means." Bob told me once that our farm was said to have been given to black people during Reconstruction. (I don't know about this; I doubt that it is true, but my twelve-year-old brother believed it, and at the time that was enough for me.) There were many tales of people who had lost their land, and, as in the medieval Europe I have already compared it to, in the South being landless signified a lack of caste that struck ice into the soul. The droves of people moving down from the hills every year during the Depression were living examples of a condition so terrible to us that we could hardly imagine it. The ones who came from the hills, didn't stick in the Delta, and went on to California were the most frightening of all. They were *really rootless*. The land itself was more than a busines, a way to make a living. It was a part of our idea of who and what we were.

My great-grandfather came to Arkansas sometime before 1841 and acquired this land in 1849. The name of the Indian who relinquished it is on the abstract. As the crow flies, the farm lies some four miles west of the Arkansas River, about twenty miles northwest of the point where it runs into the Mississippi. It is about seven miles west of Arkansas Post, the oldest white settlement west of the Mississippi River, and lies between two small towns, Dumas and Watson. In 1861, my grandfather marched off to war, to try to remove his property from the United States and, after the surrender, returned to farm and pass the land along to my father, who in turn passed it to us. My nephew, son of my oldest brother, runs it now. The associations and tales that go with the long ties between my family and the land form a rich placenta for my feelings about it. The farm is the physical arena where my fantasies grew and where these things that I tell here took place or were told to me. It is the place where I began the journey to become myself.

The farm lies between Watson and Dumas, the towns where we went to school and church, ginned our cotton, and bought groceries and farm supplies. Watson was only six miles away and in the 1930s was a fairly bustling place because of the sawmills in the surrounding woods, because of the railroad crews working on the Missouri-

Pacific line that went through the middle of town on the way from New Orleans to Memphis, and because it was a farming center with a cotton gin. During the ginning season, from mid-August until December or January, cotton dominated small Delta towns like this one. There was always a line of wagons and trucks waiting a turn under the big suction pipe that took the loose cotton into the gin machinery, where the seeds were separated from the fiber and set aside and the cotton itself, less than half the bulk that had come in, was compressed into a neat, oblong bale wrapped in hemp. A good bale weighed about 1,300 pounds before ginning and about 500 after. Some people, usually those with only a few bales, sold their cotton as it was ginned. My father liked to sell all his crop at once. Everyone, however, sold the seed immediately for money to pay the pickers. Ginning season had a hopeful air about it, even in those terrible years when cotton brought next to nothing. At least during the harvest there were *glimpses* of money. Moreover, when farmers see their product go to market, it is easier to find the courage to hope that next year will be better.

Gins dominated small Delta towns in another way too. Our raised consciousness sees it now as noise pollution, but everyone was so accustomed to the steady pounding of the steam gin engine day and night for four or five months a year that it was missed when the old steam engines were replaced with electric equipment after World War II. There was an absolutely steady *bam bam bam bam* that you could hear and feel vibrate in the floor of all the buildings in town, and those old gins also put out a cloud of lint that hung in the air for at least a half a mile in every direction.

. In addition to the depot and gin, Watson at that time had five or six general stores; a liquor store; two or three service stations; two or three white churches and two or three black ones; a white school and a black one, both under the direction of the same white superintendent; a white honky-tonk and a black one, within a stone's throw of each other but as segregated as the schools and churches; a post office; and a jail. Red Fork Bayou ran through town, as did the gravel highway and the railroad track. There were no paved streets; most were not even graveled. There were fewer than a thousand people in Watson, and no rich ones. Some were better off than others, but nobody was truly wealthy. The gin belonged to a wealthy man who lived in Dumas and stayed with a family out near the river during the week to oversee his plantations and ginning business. Women in Watson went to weekly meetings of the Missionary Society and monthly meetings of the Home Demonstration Club. This club for rural women was sponsored by the County Extension Service of the Department of Agriculture and taught women how to sew, can, decorate their homes, and make do with whatever they had. I can remember only one household where bridge was regularly played, and it was a struggle to get two tables of players together.

Dumas, twelve miles west of the farm, was larger, with a population of around 2,500. It too had the railroad running through the middle of town, but more businesses (four or five cotton gins, ten or fifteen stores), numerous churches, the usual black and white schools, and some rich people. Because of its prosperity, it had a different social structure; women played bridge and went to garden clubs as well as to the Missionary Society. There were doctors in Dumas, and by my time, a hospital. There was a country club a few miles out of town on a lake, where high-school parties were held privately because the Baptists in town would not tolerate the school's sponsoring dances, although they allowed their children to go to the private events. It was in the transfer to the Dumas school that I learned the importance of not being "common." As soon as the town kids in the seventh grade learned from their parents who my family was, and that our house was painted white, I was accepted. Country children who were not accepted had a hard row to hoe. A friend whose family bought a farm and moved there told me forty years later that she would never forget her first day at school in Dumas, when one of the town girls stopped her on the stairs and said, "Now, did you say your house is painted white?" Fortunately, it was, so she was on the inside track. Poor people's houses, the houses of sharecroppers and smaller renters, were not painted at all. Seldom did children from those houses get invited anywhere.

There had been a time when Watson was a more thriving center than Dumas, first because of its proximity to the river and later because it was on the New Orleans-to-Memphis train route. However, when the north-south federal highway arrived, it went through Dumas, which was on higher ground, while Watson and the older towns, which were likely to be flooded, were left aside.

The church my family had been attached to for years was the Methodist Church in Watson. We also went to school in Watson until 1943, when the only school-age brother left and I transferred to the Dumas school. Until that time, I suspect that I probably had not been to Dumas more than a hundred times in the eleven years of my life, and those trips had been primarily to see the doctor. I never became very attached to either of those towns. While in high school, I had close friends in Dumas and for a while wanted to spend all my time there. But my deepest attachment was to the land we lived on, and to the ryhthm of farming life.

The whole matter of my upbringing is fraught with ironies. It is significant that I don't live on that land now. I needed to leave it as much as I needed to go find conversation rather than stories. But I was made whole by some of the very things that tore me apart. For example, the snobbishness that rotted the possibility of friendships which might have relieved my terrible loneliness as a child gave me the confidence as an adult to go anywhere and do anything I wanted to do, once I understood that I could not bear to stay there. For I have never doubted the notion I was given then that people who own land and are not common can do anything. The Delta of the mind had its effect. Indeed it did. And yet, so mixed are my feelings about it that what I write here, like nine-tenths of the writing that southerners do, is an attempt to explain the ambivalence behind the epigraph I have chosen for this book, from William Faulkner's *Absalom, Absalom!* After months of speculation about the nature of the South and therefore of himself, Quentin Compson is still surprised at what comes out when his Canadian roommate forces him to sort out his feelings. When Shreve asks, "Why do you hate the South?," I think that Quentin's answer is not the denial, even to himself, that his words imply. There is speculation, even wonder in his answer, if one reads it aloud, emphasizing as Faulkner does. After meeting the thought, perhaps for the first time in his life, he says quickly, without emphasis because it is unthinkable, "I don't hate it." Then, when the possibility hits home and must be denied, "I dont hate it," he says. "*I dont hate it* he thought, panting in the cold air, the iron New England dark: *I dont. I dont! I dont hate it! I dont hate it!*" This is the ambivalence at the heart of southern identity.

2

The Household

The house I grew up in was full of people. There were my parents, four brothers, a sister, my father's sister Sally, and me, to begin with. This basic crowd was joined from time to time by visiting relatives, preachers who came to hold the Methodist revival each summer, and their wives. Then, from 1938 through 1942, we boarded a schoolteacher. Fortunately the house was large, but more fortuitous was the abundance of space around it that made up for the crowd in it; and even more beneficial than this for our growth was my parents' penchant for leaving their children alone. There were the usual barns, sheds, and corn cribs necessary to accommodate the horde of animals needed to supply the family with meat and milk and provide the mule power for the farming operation. Barns and cribs to . play in have been the salvation of many a lonely country child, but in addition to these, we had, within fifty yards of our back door, a living, seething swamp for our personal entertainment. It never seemed to occur to anyone that it might not be a good idea to let small children play in a swamp infested with thousands of poisonous snakes, possibly because snakes were so much a part of the scenery that nobody paid them any mind. I have never seen them in such concentration in any other place except the snake house at the St. Louis zoo. They were swimming or sunning themselves on logs and tree limbs everywhere you looked in that swamp. When I was very young, there was a rotten old scow around that the older boys had built, and before we got in it, we were careful to chase out the cottonmouth moccasins that liked to hide under the seats. We also had

Margaret Jones Bolsterli
at seventeen.

The Jones family in 1901. Counter-clockwise from lower left: Frierson
Jones Stroud, Irene Walton Jones Stroud, Sarah Virginia Jones (Aunt Sally),
unidentified woman, Joseph Calvin Stroud, Margaret Amanda Jones, Ruth Stroud,
Joseph Hubbard Jones, Gordon Hubbard Jones, Grover Cleveland Jones (author's
father), Luther Jones, and Charlie Howell (a neighbor.)

Aunt Sally posing with
Uncle Luther's rifle, about 1898.

Zena Cason Jones
and Margaret in 1932.

The Jones family in 1932.

Pauline Jones Lloyd
and a school friend in 1934.

The author in 1985.

to be careful about paddling under overhanging limbs, because in their fright snakes had been known to roll off into the boat.

Some of those snakes were four feet long and three inches thick. Moccasins are extremely shy, however, and we learned early that they were as scared of us as we might be of them. A good chicken game was to see who could let an unsuspecting snake swim closest to a bare foot dangling down the bank to the edge of the water. The closest I could stand to let one come to my foot was about twenty-four inches. You sat very still until you couldn't bear it getting any closer and then all you had to do was twitch your foot and the terrified snake would rise straight up and fall over backwards getting away. We believed that they would not bite under water. Whether true or not, this idea was comforting, because there were times when the boat sank or we were gigging frogs or something and absolutely had to be in the water ourselves. None of the children ever got bitten playing in the swamp. Ironically, the only person in the family ever to suffer snakebite was Mother, who was mortally afraid of them anyway. One day before I was born, she put her hand under a sweet-potato vine in the garden and a rattlesnake bit it. There was nobody at home to take her to the doctor. The only person near was an old woman who grabbed a chicken and cut it open alive and told Mother to stick her hand in the warm body of the dying chicken "to draw out the poison." Apparently it did; the hand swelled to twice its normal size and my mother was sick for a few days, but that was the end of it.

My brother Ted had a twenty-two rifle that we used to shoot snakes and turtles by the thousands—hard to believe though that may be. A cousin and I shot several hundred in one week, one summer. The brothers taught me to shoot by the time I was eight, and when I was ten, I was allowed to take the twenty-two out alone, more for protection against the drunken, sex-crazed men thought to be lurking behind every bush than for protection against snakes, I suspect. When the old boat finally sank for good, Bob and I spent the first few weeks of several summers building a raft that we never got

to float with us on it. There were so many willows that nobody
minded if we chopped a few down; they seemed to grow back as
fast as we felled them. In fact, willows held so tenaciously to life that
when the tenants used them as corner posts for chicken houses and
privies, they would sprout and there would be four little trees holding up the roof of the structure. Our raft would sprout from summer
to summer even before we gave up trying to make it float.

Equal in importance to the literal space we grew up in was the
tremendous amount of figurative space that was allowed us; there
was no concerted effort to keep up with anybody. If I chose to disap-
pear for a few hours, I knew that a search would not be in progress
when I turned up. This certainty gave me room in which to *be*, and
I believe that communion with that primeval swamp put me in a
special relationship with the earth. The swamp is eternal in its continual decay and renewal, and there are creatures in it with millions
of years of continuity. Not alligators (we were a little too far north
for that), but grinnells, gars, turtles, snakes, mussels, and lizards, not
to mention algae and some extremely primitive birds as well as the
usual run of Deep-South insects that, I believe, without the advent
of chemicals would have inherited the earth by now and may do
so yet. The gar is a long, round, ugly, primitive fish with an enor-
mous mouth and huge teeth. The grinnell, or bowfin, defined by
ichthyologists as a living fossil, is practically indestructible and will
burrow into the mud and live on after a swamp is essentially dry.
And ours was a small swamp that dried up most years to a pond,
about thirty feet in diameter and eight inches deep at the center,
called the gar hole. As the water surface shrank in July and August,
the remnants of swamp life retreated to this slimy, stinking, moss-
and algae-filled puddle to try to keep alive until the fall rains. The
gar hole drew our attention in spite of its indescribable smell, for,
as it got smaller and smaller, that pond became the essential primor-
dial swamp, the center of things, the beginning. It had in it the noises
of bullfrogs, insects, birds, and constantly-flopping gars. Cranes would
stand dejectedly on one foot waiting for minnows. (When I was

small I thought they probably stood on one foot because the water was so filthy they couldn't bear to put both of them down.) Cranes, so beautiful and graceful at a distance, up close appear so awkward and dirty that I have always felt distaste for eating white chickens because they remind me of cranes.

As the floor of the swamp dried, we could walk all over it to find the mussel shells that we were sure would one day yield a pearl. Tiny frogs hopped in every direction, like grasshoppers in an open field, and there were chinquapins to be found and eaten. Chinquapins are little nuts that grow in swamps and are distinguished by having, in addition to a minute edible white nutmeat, another green nutmeat of equal size said to be deadly poison. We were careful not to eat the green part, and it was the freedom to make such decisions without adult interference that I see as having been such a gift. I do not know whether those green bits were poisonous or not, but we thought they were and learned to exercise caution for ourselves. It was the equivalent of a city child's learning to cross a busy street alone. Cousin Albert, the daredevil among us, once terrified the group by eating a green bit, but, since he carefully washed it down with castor oil, nobody could say whether it was poison or not. The only thing certain was that he had more nerve than most. (This was a fact never in doubt; at fifteen he walked across the Arkansas River at Little Rock on the catwalk under the railroad bridge carrying my ten-year-old brother Bob on his shoulders.)

I also believe that being alone in a place where absolutely the only sounds were the sounds of nature gave a special part of our inner resources a chance to develop. In late fall, when the frogs and snakes had gone to sleep and the song birds had flown even farther south, there was a silence so profound in that swamp that you felt yourself a part of nature rather than something outside it; you seemed actually to be breathing with it. I think this communion with nature was what William Blake meant by seeing through the eye and not with it. I who have always had a tendency to stand to one side and observe life, who was an observer even while having babies by natural childbirth, probably have never felt myself more a part of nature than I did in the steaming childhood summers and winter silences of that swamp.

We would hear the geese go over in fall and spring and go out in the night to see those long V-formations against the sky (I have always heard them, even in cities like St. Louis and Minneapolis, above the late-night traffic noises). At two o'clock one winter morning, Bob and I separately knew that a rare snow was falling, got up, put on our clothes, and went out into the eerie white swamp to see the snow make strange shapes of the cypress knees and button willows. I remember how pure it all was in that pale light.

And then there were the people in the house, the people who made it different from houses that had only the requisite parents and children. There was the oldest, Aunt Sally, my father's oldest sister, who had devoted her life to taking care of him. The year she went away to college, he fell and broke his leg playing baseball. Set wrong by a drunk doctor, the leg did not heal properly, so she came home to help with him for a semester and never left. When my mother married him, he had never even washed his own hair, so extensive was Aunt Sally's care. She was a strong-minded woman who had to be listened to, because some of the land our living depended on belonged to her. Although she did not care for my brothers and would not let them come into her room, she adored my sister and me and spent hours upon hours with us. It was she who told me one quiet evening that the owl in the swamp was saying, "Whooo, whoooo, who cooks for you all?" In the limited circumstance of that community, she had been something of a belle in her day and would let me play with her old clothes and jewelry. One morning when I was about five, I was in her room, sitting at a little table, an old fox stole with amber-colored glass eyes around my neck, playing with a little gold pendant watch given her by some long-gone beau ("Absence makes the heart grow fonder" is engraved in the back of the case; she left it to me in her will). Aunt Sally was sweeping the floor and humming a tune, when suddenly she dropped the broom, threw her hands to her head, screamed, "Oh, Zena, please help me," and fell across the bed. My mother rushed in, but there was nothing to be done. It was the first sign of the brain tumor that killed her within a year. I recall that, at the funeral, some dark shadow of a woman I can no longer identify told me that if I felt like crying, the closet under the stairs would be a good place for it. The closet was too dark; I declined and did not cry for years after. Thus was one more stiff upper lip forged. But the moment of that scream is engraved on my memory in sepia, like an old photograph, with the odor of mothballs from the fox around my neck. She had wanted to be a painter and showed talent; several of her oils still hang in the house.

One visitor we had every summer for years was Cousin Cassie, an ancient, distant cousin of Daddy's who had been forced by indigence to go live with a daughter in Beaumont, Texas. She existed for the month or so she spent with us every year and was no trouble that I remember, except that she was not a reader and she dipped snuff. Nice people did not dip snuff; it was unthinkable that anyone in our house should do such a thing, but she did. Dipping snuff is not a matter of sniffing it in the refined, eighteenth-century fashion for the delicious pucker in the nostrils; it is a matter of taking a little stick and tamping the snuff between the lower lip and gum so the nicotine can get into the bloodstream by osmosis. It requires a great deal of spitting, and as snuff dippers age, they tend not to notice occasional little runnels of juice trickling down their chins. Their speech is affected also, because of the effort it takes to shape words with a mass of snuff in your lip. Bob and I would mix cocoa and sugar to make "snuff" which we dipped while pretending we were confirmed users. He was a good mimic and could "do" Cousin Cassie perfectly.

Mother hated the snuff, but she hated it even more that Cousin Cassie did not read and so had to be talked to. Reading was a disease that possessed the rest of us. We read everything we could get our hands on, falling upon magazines like *The Saturday Evening Post* and

The Country Gentleman the minute the mailman left them. There was a rule that Daddy and Grover, my oldest brother, got first crack at everything, because they were considered the most important members of the family; after all, they ran the farm and so made the living. With the rest of us, it was catch as catch can, except that when Mother lay down for her afternoon nap, it was her prerogative to read herself to sleep with the newest material. After supper we sat around the living-room table reading by an Aladdin lamp, the only one we owned, and it gave about as much light as a hundred-watt electric bulb. But it was much brighter than the other kerosene lamps that provided light in the rest of the house. When World War II began and there was money again, Mother joined the Book-of-the-Month Club, and we read novels. We also read the *Arkansas Gazette* and *The McGehee Times*, the county newspaper. One thing we did not read was *The Grit*, a weekly paper peddled in rural areas all over the country. Not only was the news old by the time *The Grit* got to us, but also it was considered somewhat lower class and only for people who could not afford fresher news. "Poor" people read *The Grit*. We did not have any money, but compared to most people around us, we were definitely not "poor." I suspect that when Mother used the term "poor," she really meant "common."

We were all readers except Ted, who would not even read the books for his school reports. So Mother read aloud and made him listen. She read well, and I remember identifying with Maggie Tulliver when she read *The Mill on the Floss*, one of the books forced on Ted and enjoyed by the rest of us. She had taken elocution lessons in college and sometimes gave us "readings" she had learned there. These were sentimental, melodramatic poems that would either drive Bob to tears or make him writhe with embarrassment. My favorite began "Poor little butterfly, dead on the walk/Pick him up, Rose, with a violet stalk" and progressed through the funeral and interment of the deceased. Mother was a firm believer in the inspirational value of the printed word and offered fifty cents to the first one of the younger children who memorized "The Psalm of Life." Bob took the prize, but to this day I can quote several stanzas and suspect that this exercise in bathos may have had a strong influence on me. "Let us then be up and doing with a heart for any fate/Still achieving, still pursuing" was not a bad line to teach an eight-year-old in the South in the middle of the Great Depression.

In absolute terms, my father was better educated than many college graduates, although all his formal schooling had been limited to a one-room school. He spoke well, wrote a clear hand, and, like Mother, had a deep respect for education and wanted us to have as much of it as we could get. He was bitter because his older sisters, and perhaps even his brothers, had been sent to live with relatives in Tennessee to go to school, but since the family could not bear to part with him, the baby, he was not allowed to go. He had not particularly wanted to be a farmer; it had simply fallen to him, and he was not equipped to do anything else. He and Mother conveyed their respect for education to us by their interest in the printed word, to which we quite simply became addicted. This meant that a nonreader stuck in that household disrupted the natural flow of things. It was a burden that somebody would have to talk with Cousin Cassie when there was something new to read.

Fortunately, Daddy did not like to read on summer evenings because the heat of the lamp made the house even more suffocating and attracted bugs small enough to get through the screens. He preferred to sit on the dark porch smoking cigarettes and brooding about the crop that he always thought was failing. Cousin Cassie loved to sit out there with him, brooding and dipping snuff. Since she was of his parents' generation, they had stories in common that went back before his birth. A favorite subject of theirs concerned the way "the country is opening up." Which meant that woods were being cleared for lumber and the land was being turned into rich farms. Roads were being built where there had been mud lanes before, and a few dreamers were already talking about someday paving our road that so recently had been graveled. Before the gravel was put down in 1931, that road had been so bad that until 1927 it was easier to ship cotton on steamboats on the river and receive supplies at a dock four miles away than to get to a town. At that time my family, like most with sizable farms, had been forced to keep a small commissary to provide for the people on the place.

Part of the reason for the country's opening up in the thirties was an influx of people from the hills who moved down to the rich Delta and took up land that the natives had neither the will nor the energy to farm. Farmland in the hills wore out just as the Depression hit, and the combination of these factors drove the marginal hill farmers to look for opportunity elsewhere. The Delta looked like paradise to them, because rich, black bottomland called "buckshot" or "gumbo" could be bought for a dollar an acre and back taxes. This meant that a family could buy forty acres for less than two hundred and fifty dollars, and in addition, the government would lend money for the purchase. There had never been many white people in Desha County, and suddenly there were hundreds of new families of independent, hardworking, ambitious, hungry white people who desperately wanted to better their situation by owning land. They seemed like people from Mars to the Deltans, because they spoke a different dialect, worked so hard, and were poor in a way that white people in the Delta seldom were. But open up the country they did.

Anyway, Cousin Cassie's visits were useful in one way because, without her to keep Daddy company, Mother would have felt compelled to sit out there on the porch with him when she preferred to be inside reading. When I conjure up my mother's presence, she is doing one of two things: reading, usually lying down with her feet hanging over the side of the couch or bed, or doing what she called "fancy work" (intricate drawn-work lace) or embroidery. She had had two years of college when "fancy work" and elocution were considered essential for a girl's education. (I was to be sent to her old college because she had enjoyed it so much and, I suspect, because she harbored a faint hope that they would teach me to make lace, since she had been unable to direct my interest to it.) Mother came to the community to teach in the one-room school. She had grown up on a hard-acre farm at Fountain Hill, some thirty miles west, as the crow flies, but culturally much further away because it is ouside the Delta. Her father, Grandpa Albert Gallatin Cason, had come to Arkansas by accident. An adolescent at the end of the Civil War, he was hanging around the railroad yard at Vicksburg, Mississippi, and inadvertently got locked up in a boxcar that was not opened until the train reached Monticello, Arkansas, where he emerged and decided to stay. He felt there was nothing to go back to Mississippi for. His father was dead, and his family's large plantation near what is now called Yazoo City, Mississippi, unfortunately had lain in the line of march of the Union Army and been burned to the ground. Preferring new territory to scorched earth, he convinced his mother to sell the Mississippi property and buy a farm at Fountain Hill. This woman, "Little Grandma," lived with my mother's family until her death and was the root of pride, manners, and ambition in Mother. Grandpa Cason farmed until past midlife, when he felt called to the Methodist ministry and became a circuit rider. It was told that, at the age of seventy, he was still agile enough to jump into the air and click his heels together before hitting the ground again. His childhood companion, a black youth brought up as his personal slave, was locked up in that boxcar, too, but nobody ever told what became of him. There were no black people around my mother's household during her childhood, and she never got used to them. She believed that the prevailing treatment of blacks in the Delta was terrible, but she felt powerless in the face of it. She told that, soon after she came to the community to teach, at dusk one evening a black woman rattled the gate and asked to speak to Miss Cason. Mother went out, and the woman, whom she had never seen before, began to cry and said that she had come to tell Mother that she had gotten religion and no longer hated her. She was the teacher at the local black school and, Mother thought, undoubtedly was paid less and had even poorer facilities than Mother had and so had been envious of her. It was a scene my mother never forgot.

Mother was one of the shyest people I have ever met, a genuine recluse who seldom left the house except to go to church. I do not remember ever seeing her in a store. My father bought groceries and everything else from a detailed list she made for him. She sewed beautifully and made clothes for herself, my sister Pauline, and me and nurtured a sense of style by reading women's magazines. When she got older and no longer felt like sewing, she would write to the "personal shopper" at department stores in Little Rock, describing the clothes she wanted, and a selection would be sent to give her a choice. She would keep what she liked and mail back the things she didn't want. But I remember her reading more than sewing or making lace, for if reading was a disease in all of us, in her it was a raging fever. I do not remember her ever discussing what she read; I believe she did it purely for escape. This understanding of her character was thirty years in coming to me and was partly arrived at by understanding, finally, her attitude towards me.

For my shy, reclusive mother, who never complained about her stultifyingly dull situation in life, harbored the most exciting ambitions for me that she could imagine. In the first place, she told me from the beginning that I was smart enough and capable of doing anything I wanted to do and that I should leave because my talents could never be fully realized there. The best thing for me to do, she thought, would be to go to Alaska, because it was the last frontier and I had qualities that would flourish in that atmosphere. Teaching was the only way she could think of for me to manage it, so she advised me to get a teaching certificate and go. This, from a woman locked in a tradition that forbade women to be independent or teach their daughters to want independence, was remarkable. Mother was forty-two when I was born and even then worn out by hard work and motherhood. (She had help with the laundry and usually with the housework but never a cook, and during crop seasons, even the women she counted on for help around the house were lost to the fields.) By the time I was in high school, she was a semi-invalid from poorly defined and wrongly diagnosed illnesses for which the cures almost killed her. But I believe that she also took to her bed from boredom, frustration, and despair. She must have realized that if the family achieved everything hoped for in the way of financial security, her situation would hardly be altered at all. And judging from the encouragement she gave me to get out of there, it was definitely not a situation she recommended.

My mother was not an affectionate woman, yet I remember sitting on her lap at an age when we were both teased about it because I was so big. She would laugh and say that she would hold a child on her lap until its feet could drag the floor. I do not remember nursing, but I do remember being weaned at a rather advanced age because in the attempt to divert my attention from the breast, they would produce any other food I asked for, even in the middle of the night. I recall having a hot, buttered biscuit with molasses on one such occasion, how dark the rest of the house was, and how good the biscuit tasted, handed to me as it was, in the bed. At that time it was not uncommon for southern children to be up and around before being weaned. I suspect there was a lingering hope that it constituted birth control. I do know that there was apparently discussion about the wisdom of having another child, that turned out to be me, in 1931. There was a letter in one of the trunks in the attic from a cousin in California to Aunt Sally saying she just did not know what my parents could be thinking of, doing such a thing with the country in the shape it was in. I read this letter with great resentment when I found it, as an adult.

I never knew my mother as a person – separate, that is, from the role of parent. Friends tell me of outliving the generation gap to become friends with their mothers. But mine died before this could happen, when I was twenty-three, from a stroke she suffered getting ready for my wedding. So I can only speculate about what she thought about her life and what she would make of mine. I did not take her advice and go to Alaska, but her encouragement lies behind a number of other things I have done. I think she would approve of the life I have made.

My oldest brother, Grover, twenty when I was born, was firmly

situated on the parents' side of the balance in the household between parents and children. It was ordained from his childhood that
he would be the farmer on the place one day and his training began
early, as it must, for that kind of responsibility. It was said that by
the time he was twelve, he could take a crew of hands out to build
fences or do whatever needed to be done about the place. By the
time I remember anything, he was practically in charge. I do not
know why, exactly. Something seemed to have broken my father's
spirit; I remember him as an old man, always. And others saw him
that way too. He did not drive a car, for example, and decisions about
the farm were made with Grover as equal partner. The 1927 Flood
undoubtedly had something to do with it, for in addition to washing
away the work of a lifetime, it demonstrated that the danger of another one was always there.

Another blow that may have helped to break him was the loss
in 1931 of the second son, my brother Paul, who died of rheumatic
fever a few months after I was born. Paul was a shining boy, adored
by everybody, and they never got over losing him. He was in the
household conversation for twenty years after his death. But Grover
had always been the bright and capable first-born, whom everybody
could depend on; and after the flood he took more and more responsibility in the family. Without assuming martyrdom, he sacrificed
his youth for us the way Aunt Sally had for my father.

My beautiful sister Pauline was five years younger than Grover,
and my nurse. She took me over when I was born, and I remember
that when I was five and she was about to marry, she took me to
town to the barber to have my hair cut, since there would no longer
be anyone at home with time to make corkscrew curls. Mr. Fowler,
the barber, put a board across the arms of the barber chair for me
to sit on and gave me a "windblown bob." I did not know what was
happening until it was done, as he wisely had turned me to face the
street while he ravaged my hair. When he whirled me around to the
mirror, I wept. So Pauline married and left in 1936 and was a visitor
from then on, although she lived six miles away in Watson. Bill, the

man she married, had been around all our lives and was already in the family stories when they married, for teasing Aunt Sally, whose fear of fire was legendary. She took a bucket of water into her bedroom every night of her life, in case of fire. She also soaked down the floor under the kitchen stove every night just in case enough heat should radiate out of it to set the floor on fire. Aunt Sally "helped out" occasionally at the drugstore in Watson, and Bill was one of the kids who teased her about fires. He would bring a kerosene lamp into the store and say, "Look, Miss Sally, don't you want to see me light this lamp?" Another trick was to crawl under the drugstore and blow cigarette smoke up through the cracks and knotholes in the floor.

Jodie, the next brother, was ten years older than I and on the fence between the generations. He was a shadowy figure to me, but I have one clear memory of an act of kindness to me at school, where my brothers usually tried to ignore my existence. Because I fought so much and embarrassed them, most of the time they pretended they did not know me. But one day I was hurt and bleeding from a minor head wound when time came to board the bus for home, and Jodie made everyone stand aside and let me get on first. I still remember the waves of love and gratitude I felt at this.

Ted was next, seven years older than I, and adopted. He was really a first cousin, my mother's nephew whose own mother had died in childbirth. He came to live with us shortly after he was born and was so much one of us that if his name had been the same, I doubt that I ever would have known that he was not my brother. His father was still alive, however, and did not want him to give up his name. I had more in common with Ted than with my own siblings and in occasional spasms of self-pity would suspect that I too had been found in some other woodpile. Ted was as determined as I was, by a fairly early age, to leave there; we both liked a good time, which I think the others did not, and he was as little touched by the religiosity of the household as I was.

Bob, five years older than I, was my hero. He would allow me to go with him wherever he happened to be going if I caused no trouble and did exactly as he said. Walking through woods, I had to be prepared to walk as silently as an Indian and respond to his hand signals to tell me when to stop or start walking again. I was as well trained as a circus seal. This was the way we were always going to slip up on the squirrels he intended to shoot with the twenty-two. He took me fishing and hunting and filled my head with all kinds of lore and family history. I remember his explanation of the way a whiskey still worked when we came across the ruins of one deep in the swamp. I loved Bob and he loved me, but we fought with a devotion that may be possible only between children who are so fond of each other.

A photograph taken of the children when I was about three tells more than it shows. Grover is not in it; he was undoubtedly taking the picture. Pauline has cut herself out because she was dissatisfied with the way she looked. Jodie is on his knees to keep from being taller than Ted and Bob. And those two are lovingly but firmly holding me by the arms to keep me from stepping on the baby ducks that were waddling around our feet. The ducks aren't in the picture either, but we all remember they were there and they claim that as usual I was trying to step on them.

This was the nuclear family. But numerous cousins came to spend the summers with us. Joe Junior Stroud, and Sonny and Jimmy Saine on my father's side; Albert Campbell and Randall Cason on Mother's. (I especially remember Randall's summer with us, because I was about three years old and he would let me stand between his knees and drive Grover's Model A Ford.) Somebody else, whose identity I cannot remember, was there one summer because he had killed a man and, although acquitted by a jury, was thought to be safer away from his home community for a while. These visiting boys did whatever my brothers were doing in the fields and woods. Another young man, Clyo Moore, after trouble with his stepfather, came to live with us for a few years, then married and lived on the place with his wife for over thirty years.

Then, in addition to all these people in and out of the house, in

1938, when I was seven, Jodie graduated from high school and there was no money to send him to college. Mother came up with the obvious solution: we would board a Watson teacher. Boarding a teacher was a respectable way to make a little money while providing the community with a needed service, as there were no apartments to be had. (In fact, since my grandfather's house had been the regular boarding place for the teacher at the local one-room school for some fifty years, it was as a boarder in his house that Mother had come there in 1908 and met my father.) So we added a teacher to the number in the house, a woman named Mary Myrtle Jones from Port Gibson, Mississippi ("Pote Gibson" as Bob mimicked her pronunciation). She was not related to us but became a member of the family in a matter of weeks, because of a passion she and Mother shared. They were both grammar nuts. They thought that the barbarians were at the door and the English language was crumbling around us. I have mentioned that the hill people spoke a different dialect; it was different in vocabulary, accent, and syntax, and was associated in the native Delta mind with "shiftlessness" and poverty. After all, had not these people *moved*? Nobody in the Delta moved; they stayed where they were, no matter what. It must have been tempting, if inconceivable, to leave after the 1927 Flood, not to mention other disasters such as war and Reconstruction. True, pieces of our land had been lost or sold off over the years, but the nucleus remained untouched, and nested in it was the family pride.

However, these years I am describing saw the terrifying spectacle of Americans on the move, many of whom had owned land, and we were afraid that a few bad crop years might put us on a truck to California or off to rent somebody else's land and live in somebody else's house. This fear needs to be couched in the context of our settled condition: I doubt that in the entire span of my father's seventy-two years he spent more than 365 days outside his own house, and most of that time would have been short stays in hunting camps of one kind or another. But it was a terrible fear grounded in genuine possibility, and one way to hold onto our place in the sun was seen by Mother and Miss Jones as a matter of speaking pro-per English. The issue was clear to them: the economic threat had something to do with the government, but the social threat was basi-cally a linguistic one. They were not alone, of course, and others in the community interested in retaining the status associated with good grammar were hanging on by the skin of their teeth, as they were rapidly being outnumbered by the hill people. Mother and Miss Jones were like human flies on this cliff of respectability, deter-mined to keep us all up there roped together with them, while those with poor usage and a hill accent inevitably fell off, as they must if there were justice in the world. Miss Jones would come home from school, open her first bottle of "cocola" of the day, seat herself in the big rocker, cross her legs at the knee so one tiny foot in its stiletto-heeled, open-toed, sling-back pump would swing, and enu-merate the day's assaults on the English language by some hill child. (She was less than five feet tall, dressed in the latest fashion, and wore those high heels all the time. "Honey, I just *feel* better in heels," she would say.) But where grammar was concerned, it was more than a matter of disapproval, as it was her job to figure out ways of teaching people who did not know any better, not to speak or even think in forms like, "Hit don't make me no never mind." She would say to Mother, "Oh, Mrs. Jones, *how* oh *how* can you teach a child who doesn't know *anything* not to use the double negative." And Mother would whip out paper and pencil and say, "Let's try a diagram." They both loved diagramming sentences. It represented a degree of order and logic they wanted the world to aspire to. If every-body could just be made to understand a good diagram, they thought, the rest would follow.

Double negatives were harder to deal with than the earmark of hill dialect that most of the newcomers had on arrival and lost shortly hereafter, the use of *you'uns* instead of *y'all* for the plural *you*. This locution produced contempt faster than anything else in the natives who naturally felt that *their* word *y'all* denoted status and breeding. Actually, before the hill people came, few of the natives had probably given it much thought, because a comparison with standard English happened so seldom. There were so few visitors to Desha County from parts of the world where standard English was spoken that *you* for second person plural was an oddity confined to print. No sane teacher would have tried to teach students to say *you* rather than *y'all* in this case. *You'uns* was a different matter, and its use was laughed at so openly that it was one of the first items of hill culture the new arrivals threw overboard on their way to becoming Deltans, a feat they successfully accomplished in one generation, either because the efforts of people like Mother and Miss Jones bore fruit, or because the standards disappeared. All I know is that the attention paid to grammar and pronunciation in our house resembled what I have heard about the attention paid to it for the same reason by Germans living in the Polish Corridor, who, in order to hang onto their identity, insisted that their children be taught the purest German. Grammatical speech was thought to separate the sheep from the goats; it denoted a position in the community and the world that people in my house took seriously. Mother would say to us on every possible occasion, "Never forget that you must set an example. After all, *you* have had *advantages.*"

And she was right, we had had advantages that many did not have, because there were books in our house and respect for them and the language they were written in. We lived in the backwoods in such extreme isolation that it would have been easy to feel that we were not part of the civilized world, had it not been for books and reading.

Although technically a boarder, Miss Jones lived with us from 1938 to 1942 as a member of the family. She called me "Suster," in fact, and I believe that she looked forward to coming to our house and considered it, rather than "Pote Gibson," home during those years. By 1942, Jodie had been called to the army with his college National Guard unit, Grover and Ted had been drafted, the price of cotton had gone up, and we were no longer in financial straits. So with sadness and tears, Mother told Miss Jones that she must go, and with tears she replied that she understood and would look for another place for the next school year. By the next fall my brother-in-law had been drafted too, so she moved in with Pauline for the duration. When the war ended, Miss Jones went back to Port Gibson and married her childhood sweetheart.

World War II changed our household so drastically that I cannot imagine what it would have been like without it. My parents were under continual strain and worry about the "boys." Eventually Bob was drafted into the navy, and I was left with a few years of bliss as an only child. This gave me an opportunity to know my parents better than I would have if everyone had always been there, and I am deeply appreciative of the opportunity but regret that it took a war to provide it. They were, after all, as much older than I as many grandparents are than their grandchildren. Mother said once that having me around had kept her young because she was forced to deal with the problems of youth long past the time when she would have done, without me, the final child (all in all, they had children in the public schools for thirty-six years!). However, the subjects of our conversations were so circumscribed by her limited vision of what could be talked about with a young daughter that most of the things that concern an adolescent girl were left out of our conversation. But I remember with pleasure being snowed in for a week along with my parents late in my high-school years, because we were closer that week than at any other time in my life. Snow is rare in the Delta and so seldom outlasts its welcome that it carries a special charm. We had no telephone, and since the power lines were down, for that week we had no electricity. Reduced again to kerosene lamps for light, we realized that we had been so spoiled by ten years of electricity that we could no longer read by that soft light. So we played cards. I had never seen them play cards or any other game, but that week we played cards all day and all evening, stopping only for meals. And my father, a superb raconteur who could make a trip to the mailbox interesting, told stories. The three of us seemed to feel the enchantment of our kinship for that short time in a way that we never acknowledged again.

What I have told so far here is about the immediate family, the group who lived in the house together at that particular time. But the word *family* was a concept involving the eight generations of my father's maternal family that had been on this continent, the three of his paternal family that anybody knew anything about, and at least three generations on both sides of my mother's family. Not only was all of this written down in books and Bibles, but also it was a point of reference for my parents' expectations of us. It was not that these ancestors had been rich or powerful – none had, that I recall, although one, William Frierson, Jr., had attended the Constitutional Convention in 1788. It was important that we knew *who* they were and, that being the case, we had a responsibility not to disgrace them. If you disgraced your family, it was *all of it* you shamed. A friend from South Carolina told me that whenever he left his house for whatever reason, to go to a party, to college, to Europe, anywhere, his mother would say as she kissed him, "Never forget *who you are.*" My mother seldom expressed it. She didn't have to. I *knew* that the worst thing in the world I could do was disgrace the family and how little it would take to do it. Most southern families have genealogies lying around, and the ones who don't will, as soon as they have enough money to have them traced. A few years ago I was looking at a genealogy of an acquaintance's family that traced a direct line all the way back to Charlemagne. I asked how in the world they had managed to trace the line back that far. My friend's mother took a long drag on her cigarette and as she exhaled the smoke said, "Oh, honey, they sent 'em ten dollars."

I have noticed that southerners find this business of having a family handy for starting conversations and gaining social credit. For example, I gained immediate rapport and credibility with Allen Tate, one evening in Minneapolis when I sat beside him at dinner, by asking if he happened to know any Friersons from Tennessee, since he was from the adjacent area of Kentucky. "Why, my dear lady," he said, "my very best friend at Vanderbilt was Bill Frierson. Roomed with him four years. Are you any *kin* to the Friersons?" Now I have never met any members of that branch of my father's family and hastened to tell him so, adding that I was distantly related, my great-grandmother was a Frierson. Then I heard all about the Friersons. It got the conversation off to a good, solid, trusting start. Southerners find it comforting to have the illusion that they know who it is they are talking to.

One way this pride in family was encouraged lay in the habit of passing names down. I have always been grateful for having had enough brothers to absorb the family names I did not care for, because those names have to be given to somebody. Traditionally, the first son receives the father's given name; the second son is given the mother's maiden name. Grandfathers' names need to be used too. Daughters are named for grandmothers, favorite sisters, and cousins. But if there are no sons, they are given the obligatory names, the father's name and the mother's maiden name. That is why any southern town has a sprinkling of *Mary Johns* and *Mary Toms*, and female *Ashleys* or *Dabneys*. Like many southerners who had babies at that time, my grandparents broke tradition and named my father Grover Cleveland because that worthy was the first Democrat elected to the White House after the Civil War. My parents' first child was a stillborn girl and this may have scared them into thinking that the next child might be their last so they tacked both my father's given name, Grover, and my mother's maiden name, Cason, on him, making him Grover Cason. Having done their duty, they could give the next son a name they simply liked, Paul, and then, to my sister's despair, probably because they thought it was cute and by then were confident of enough fertility to handle all the family names, they named her Pauline. The next boy took care of both grandparents' given names, Joseph Gallatin. Following him was my adopted brother Ted, who had his own family name, Theodore Adolphus Willis, Jr. Left some choice now, with all the male names taken care of, they could choose a hero to name the next boy after, and who else for this but Robert E. Lee? And then I came along and was ostensibly named for my father's mother but was also the eighth Mary Margaret in our line of the eight generations of the Frierson connection in this country. And it has been a matter of pride to me all of my life. I do not know whether it was important to us because of some peculiarity of southern culture or because it showed that the family had been stationary enough for records to be kept, but having a family, just knowing who these people were and where they had been at a certain time in our past, was valuable to us. It helped us know who we were, and this in itself is often armor against the slings and arrows of adversity.

3

Talk

Our house was full of stories and things, but I yearned for conversation and ideas. I doubt that I had a word for it before I went off to search, but I knew there was something missing, and instinctively I knew I would probably have to leave the South to find whatever it was. If there were southerners very different from the ones I knew, in this matter, I had not met them by the time I graduated from college in 1952 and went to St. Louis to graduate school. And I have been back in the South since 1968 and have not met very many since. What passes for conversation in the South is frequently evasion disguised with charm, and children are socialized to practice it as surely as little girls are subtly taught to manipulate men.

My family dealt in anecdotes and cautionary tales which, though entertaining and instructive, did not evoke real response. I wanted to be engaged in a process; I wanted to swat the ball back over the net, impossible with a good story, which is, after all, a finished drive. Stories, by drawing the attention to images and memory, hinder the exchange of information so vital to conversation, undoubtedly the reason why southerners are so adept at telling them. When there are so many topics that could get you killed, best deal in fiction and be safe. And although everybody may know it's the truth that's being told, whatever is presented in a story gets treated as fiction.

The things in our house were the flotsam of our century in one place—whatever flotsam, that is, had survived the 1927 Flood, the awesome lake of water that stretched from Cairo, Illinois, to the Gulf of Mexico and was the subject of endless stories in our family. A disaster has to be anticipated, endured, and cleaned up after to qualify as major, and the '27 Flood met all these requirements.

It had been anticipated for years, since my family lived near the point where the Arkansas River runs into the Mississippi, and so had looked for a flood every spring. Indeed, there had been so many incidents of "high water" that, like people near a volcano who pay no attention to the single trickle of lava that appears running down the mountainside and consequently are unprepared for the real eruption, the family simply found it interesting when the levee broke in 1927 and water got high enough to run into the yard. Nobody even got out of bed that night to investigate the sound of water sloshing around under the house, but at dawn a motorboat provided by the Red Cross tied up to a porch post and evacuated the family, with only the clothes they could put on, to the highest ground within fifty miles, the levee itself.

Three months later, when the family got back from Monticello, a town in the hills where they stayed with mother's sister, there was a foot of silt on the floor of the house and watermarks six feet high on the walls. The only pieces of furniture left were the few held together by pegs; the glue in everything else had come unstuck. We were left with a few old trunks, a bed, a chest of drawers, and an old mahogany secretary. My father took the legs off the secretary and used them to build a dining table; iron beds replaced the lost wooden ones except for the remaining magnificent, primitive plantation-made wood four-poster that my grandfather, my father, my brothers, and sister and finally I were all born in. I was not there yet in 1927, but I didn't have to be to know what it was like, because I've been told so often. Even at my father's wake, when I was twenty-six, I heard the man who drove the rescue boat telling about picking up survivors in the flood. He said that one of the saddest sights in the whole experience was a lone goat on a log who said "bye-bye" as they went past.

Even that house was gone by the time of my first memories at the age of two. My mother knew by 1933 that the smell of the flood could never be washed out of it. She didn't like it anyway, because the kitchen was in a separate building, and the flood damage was the excuse she had been looking for to insist on a new one. To please Aunt Sally, who lived with us, it had to be built on the same spot, so we lived in the commissary until the new house was ready. The trunks containing letters, family papers, and photographs, which had survived the flood sitting safely in the old attic, were moved to the new one, and the story of our lives went on.

In the photographs, my grandfather, veteran of every major battle fought by the Army of Tennessee, who had died in 1904, was still glaring out from what in my childhood I thought was a tintype heaven, his weak chin hidden by a fan of white whiskers. At least I came to imagine that his chin was weak, probably because of the stories told of his willingness to let the farm go to ruin while he hunted anything that moved or read anything he could get his hands on. Cotton in the field never kept him out of the woods or away from a new book. His library floated around in the house during the flood, and my mother told of drying out the books and ironing the pages so we wouldn't have to live like savages with nothing to read.

The people in the pictures and stories were as real to me as the children in my class at school, because I knew in minute detail not only what they had looked like, but also what they had said and done. Cousin Frierson, who died in 1906 from acute indigestion, was standing right at my elbow in his little belted tweed jacket and buttoned shoes every time it crossed my mind to eat a green pecan. Dead twenty-five years before I was born, he was talked about as if he had just stepped into the wings (it was impatience that killed him; he could have waited for those pecans to get ripe).

We were all together in that place, one generation mixed with the others, and who's to say that I did not hear their voices, as I was sure I did, when the wind blew hard enough in the walnut trees in the yard that my father, as a boy, had inadvertently planted by dumping a load of nuts with his little red wagon. He had hauled them from somewhere else on the place and put them there to dry for the walnut cakes that Aunt Mandy, the cook, made so well. Forgotten, they sprouted and grew, and by the time I was six the trees were at least four feet in diameter.

And who's to say I did not see a ghost in the driveway one night, as I was sure I did, whirling in the moonlight like a dust devil?

The stories and the things went together. The old dresser that hadn't soaked apart had a bottom drawer strictly reserved for sick children. You had to be too ill to go to school but well enough to be up to be allowed to look in it. That drawer was the last resort of a mother near the end of her rope to keep an irritable child busy, and it seldom failed. Among other things in it was a tomahawk so dull the victim might have been bludgeoned but hardly chopped. The Indians who left it, the Quapaws, are said to have been too amiable to have been much interested in murder, anyway. They are also the only Indians noted by the French explorers in the region for their sense of humor.

The house is built on the site of a Quapaw village, and the tomahawk, a mortar and pestle, and hundreds of arrowheads had been plowed up on the place. But there were relics of later eras too: pince-nez from God knows where, strings of beads, a tuning fork, old watches that didn't work, and a huge brass compass that did — the very compass used by my great-grandfather to survey the county when it was still wilderness. The drawer was so full that it was too heavy for a small child to open, but none would have dared try because it was clearly understood to be a privilege for the convalescent only.

A privilege for the not-quite-convalescent was to be allowed in the old Big Bed that had survived the flood. It deserved its name, for each of its massive posts must have come from a small tree. My grandfather's initials were carved on one post at the eye level of a seven-year-old. To a sick child this bed became a carriage if there were an obliging well child to sit at the foot, with legs dangling, to play coachman. My brother Bob drove me cheerfully through endless colds, measles, and chicken pox, and I remember the loneliness of mumps because, by the time I had it, he was lost to adolescence. In addition to the usual childhood diseases, children as well as adults in those years were plagued with malaria. Everybody had it. Not usually fatal, it is a debilitating disease, and, until quinine takes hold, the patient is racked with fever and chills every third day. Malaria is no longer a problem, because, at the end of World War II, the federal government decided to get rid of it by killing off a generation of anopheles mosquitoes. This was done by spraying DDT on every ditch, swamp, lake, hog wallow, and rain barrel in the Delta. They also sprayed it inside houses and under them, in what was apparently a successful operation. The effect on us of exposure to DDT on such a scale remains to be seen.

There were other stories told in our house than our own, of course. A man we knew told about going with a friend to survey some woods over close to the levee and coming up on a "greasy-spoon" cafe just about lunchtime. They went in to eat and found themselves in a room with a dirt floor and a few tables with benches, no chairs. There were even chickens wandering around among the tables, and as they took their seats, a couple of filthy children arrived to stare at them. The woman who came to take their order was barefoot, had a dip of snuff in her lower lip, and had never in her life cleaned her fingernails. He said he didn't know what to do; he was as scared to leave as he was to stay. If they walked out, somebody might take offense. He certainly didn't know what to order. But his friend saved the day. He looked around the room and said, "I'll have a boiled egg and a coconut." This became a joke around our house, of course. An example of the height of filth was always a place where you would be willing to eat only a boiled egg and a coconut.

As I said, I yearned for ideas. I'd heard enough stories to last a lifetime by the time I went north and met people who conversed. I remember how exciting it was to say something, anything, and have something pertinent said right back without any crabwise movements. I also recall my shock at hearing, for the first time in my life, "nice" people say, "That's not true" and "I don't believe you." I was innocent of this gambit, because objective truth is so irrelevant to higher, fictional truth that nobody in my family would have dreamed of sacrificing a story to it. It was also bad manners to contradict anyone. Where I came from, responses were supposed to begin with *and*, not *but*, the respondent then taking the story a step further, where it might be subtly altered to reflect a different perception of the truth. The function of the listener was to help the process along, not to bring it to a halt with differing views. This is why northerners are considered abrasive; their normal pattern of talking requires that they begin thinking of exceptions to every generalization the minute they hear it. The mark of a good conversationalist to them concerns the number of salient, sometimes contrary points he can make, not the wit by which a southern talker is judged. And many southerners would as soon read an encyclopedia as talk to a person who does not know how to tell a story. This tradition undoubtedly has a lot to do with the reason why this region with the highest rate of illiteracy in the country has produced a disproportionate number of good writers. The association of things, people, and places with stories leads to a literary habit of mind, even among people who cannot read. In this tradition, people have a simultaneous double response to everything that happens. They respond to the event itself, while at the same time noting how it can be told. And retold. They will listen to the same story year after year at family gatherings, because it is familiar. These stories become more real than the events they chronicled to start with. Significantly, writing and certain kinds of music are the only arts to have been so nurtured in the region; it would not take the fingers of one hand to enumerate the outstanding painters from the South.

While I remember the pleasure and stimulation of my early conversations in St. Louis, how alive I felt, how intelligent, I think it is significant that I do not remember a single thing we talked about, while I have an appropriate story from my childhood attached to practically every human situation I can think of.

4

Violence

One of the photographs in the trunk is of my handsome Uncle Luther, my father's oldest brother, standing in front of a saddled horse with a deer rifle propped at an angle on his right thigh, his finger on the trigger. His hat is pushed back from his forehead and there is a slight smile on his face, which is too young to have much character. I was grown before I realized that this picture is an enlarged segment of another photograph, in the same trunk, of a group of men in a deer camp. They are assembled, standing and sitting, with their hounds and the black men who helped with the hunt, in front of the day's kill, a row of bucks hanging head down in the back of the picture. Since Uncle Luther stands at the extreme left, it was easy to cut him off the group, or rather, to cut the others away from him as may have been the intent. For one of the other hunters is his brother-in-law, Alfred Stroud, who murdered Uncle Luther in cold blood and had to leave the community. Another is Uncle Gordon, my father's older brother, who precipitated the fight.

I have tried to explain to northern friends the peculiar quality of violence that lies just under the surface of even the most civilized parts of southern society. They try to show me they understand by bringing up the dangers of city streets in New York and Detroit. But urban violence, random killing, is not what I am talking about, although the South has plenty of that, too. The sociologist John Shelton Reed, in a chapter of his book *One South* perceptively titled "Below the Smith and Wesson Line," cites the Federal Bureau of Investigation's Uniform Crime Reports of 1972 to illustrate this point.

Hunting camp, about 1898. Luther Jones stands at extreme left; Gordon Jones, third from right; Alfred Stroud, extreme right.

In that year, Atlanta had the highest number of homicides per 100,000 population in the country and was followed on the list by Gainesville, Florida; Greenville, South Carolina; and Little Rock, Arkansas. The first northern city to make the list was New York City, in ninth place! But when I speak of this other kind of violence, I beg comparison with rural areas of the Middle West, Northeast, or Northwest. There is a possibility in the South that violence will occur at any time, in any place – a possibility that I do not believe exists to such an extent in those other areas.

Since I have always been interested in why this should be, I was struck by Professor Reed's explanation in "Below the Smith and Wesson Line," because it puts my own experience in the context of normal expectation. He says that certain kinds of violence are acceptable and that southern children are simply so acculturated to this that by the time they are grown, they do not even recognize theirs as a particularly violent society. His students at the University of North Carolina, for example, when faced with statistics like those quoted above, tend to deny that the South is especially violent. I believe his argument because I was so acculturated. I recall an incident on a school bus when I was small, in which a high-school boy drew a knife and stabbed another boy's leg to the bone because he was teasing him. It was expected that he would react in such a way to persistent ridicule. Along the same line of violence that I knew about, the father and brother of one of my high-school classmates were shot to death after a tavern brawl in Dumas, and nobody bothered to clean the blood off the street. The man who shot them was let go by a jury convinced the act was done in self-defense. They were all armed, of course. Furthermore, between 1939 and 1943, two school buildings at Watson were mysteriously burned in the night, probably by somebody who just wanted to see the fire. Last summer I hired a local jack-of-all-trades to dig a sewer line on my farm with his backhoe. While he was there, I asked if he had a bulldozer with which he could dredge the creek. He had owned such a machine up until the past week, he told me, and would soon own it again.

He had sold it to a fellow down the road who used it only once, to move some gravel for a neighbor. When the job was finished, a bottle was produced, and they began to drink and talk about their war experiences. And then "them old boys" got to arguing about whose war had been more honorable, World War II or the Korean conflict. Finally, the World War II veteran said such harsh things about the business in Korea that the owner of the bulldozer reached in his pickup for his shotgun, took aim across the hood, and shot the other man to death. Since the bulldozer had not been paid for, it would revert to its original owner, and then he could clean out the creek. Southern farmers routinely carry firearms in their pick-ups, and those guns are not for show; they are there "in case of trouble." College boys carry their guns to college with them; few years pass at a southern university without somebody getting shot, or at least shot at. For some reason, it is not easy to convince these students that they do not live on a frontier and so must abandon the mores that went with the frontier mode of life. The general run of violence that Americans accept is so much worse in the South, in fact, that I am afraid to drive on rural roads in Arkansas and Missis-sippi, when I would not give fear a second thought on such roads in Wisconsin or New Hampshire. And I am not alone in my con-cern; V.S. Naipaul, in *A Turn in the South*, mentions that he was told in New York of motoring organizations that route their members on "safe" roads in the South.

But to understand this acculturation to violence, perhaps one needs to have heard as a child a soft, gentle, sad voice like my mother's, using the same tone she might use to say we were having peas for dinner, telling some story like Uncle Luther's in answer to a child's question about who that man in the picture is:

> Honey, that's your Uncle Luther. He died before I came here and mar-ried your father. It was a tragedy. You know, Uncle Alfred, Aunt Irene's husband—Aunt Irene was your father's oldest sister—drank [as if the rest of the men in that family didn't], and one time he had been gone from home for three days, and your grandfather sent your Uncle Luther

to look for him. Well, he found him all right, in a saloon in Red Fork, and talked him into coming home to his wife and children. Well, Luther got him out of that saloon, out to the horses, and when he thought Alfred was mounting his horse, he turned to climb into his own saddle. He had his left foot in the stirrup and was starting to swing himself up, when suddenly Alfred drew his hunting knife and stabbed him in the back. They say his liver was cut almost in two.

The casual recounting of a violent tale like this has a way of creating a consciousness in a child in which violence has as definite a place as the darkness under the bed which has to be leapt over every night. Furthermore, how could violence not be acceptable when corporal punishment was used so readily, both at home and in school? While I was in high school, between 1944 and 1948, it was still customary in small-town schools for the superintendent to whip boys with a strap. In prisons, adults were beaten routinely, and everybody knew it! The possibility of violence was all around, and we were accustomed to it. As John Shelton Reed remarks, the words of country-western songs attest to the acceptability of "justifiable" violence. Two of the songs he cites are "The Coward of the County" and "A Boy Named Sue." In both, a man is forced to prove his manhood by engaging in a bloody fight for revenge. In the first one, the hero must avenge the gang-rape of his wife by three brothers in the neighborhood; in the second, a man engages his father in a bloody fight for giving him a girl's name. Professor Reed does not go into the sexual implications of these two songs. But the fear of rape was one of the strongest forces shaping the lives of southern girls and women during my childhood. It lay behind my father's fear of letting me drive the twelve miles to Dumas alone, once I had a driver's license.

The possibility of this kind of violence was implied in the warnings about where women could go, especially unaccompanied, and provided definite limits to their freedom to move about, and therefore to their expectations. When I consider the freedom with which I was allowed to roam around the farm, including that swamp, I can reach only one conclusion: I was allowed this freedom because I was thought to be protected, within the boundaries of the farm, by my family's power. I was the boss's daughter. I was also considered safe on the public road while riding my horse in the neighborhood. However, outside the narrow confines where my father and brothers had power lay the domain of what I came to think of in later years as "The Drunken Sex-Crazed Negro" thought to be lurking behind every shrub in the South. "He" was always there, in the shadows of our imaginations if nowhere else. His omnipresence in the minds of white people may go a long way toward explaining the virulent nature of southern racism – it was, after all, black *men* that everybody feared. Nobody was afraid of black women; they were invited into white houses to cook and raise the children. But the fear that white womanhood, and therefore white men's pride, might be sullied by black men was a social institution as powerful as the concept of *common*. I doubt that very many white women were raped by black men. A black man indeed would have had to be crazy to do such a thing in the face of certain swift and terrible retribution. The only actual rape I ever heard about in those days was the rape of a white schoolmate by a white man she knew very well. But, as with other forms of violence common enough in all of America, rape has different connotations in the South because of the special circumstances of southern culture. The exaggerated fear of that "Drunken Sex-Crazed Negro" increased the height of the pedestal on which white women were placed (or onto which they climbed) for protection from him.

As for the only violence in my own family that I ever heard anything about, I was haunted by the story of Uncle Luther and its ramifications, and Mother would go on with it in answer to questions:

Grief over that tragedy killed Irene and left the children to be raised in your grandfather's house, and it was the same grief that finally just broke your grandmother's heart and drove her into the grave. When I first came here, you know, Aunt Mandy used to be the cook, but she was old, she was left over from slavery; by that time she was too old to cook but not too old to talk, so she used to visit with me a lot. Well,

Aunt Mandy told me that one day just before your grandmother died, she looked over from her house and saw your grandmother pacing up and down the yard wringing her hands. So Aunt Mandy came to see what the matter was. "Oh, Aunt Mandy," she said, "Alfred killed Luther and now Irene's gone and left these little children; what in the world is to become of them? What will we do?" And within a week she was dead, worried to death, I have no doubt.

Uncle Alfred's tuning fork was in the bottom drawer of the big dresser. He'd had such a fine voice, they all said, that he was in demand at weddings, funerals, and revival meetings. Everybody thought it such a shame that he had had to run away, such a fine man except for the drinking. What Mother gave me was the official family version of the story; I did not wonder about the logistics of the murder until a long time later, when I heard a different account. I was down there a few years ago interviewing elderly people for a local history project, and one of the people I talked to was Miss Hattie Hundley, who had outlived the rest of my father's generation by more than thirty years. Her family, the Irbys and Coopwoods, had been close friends of my grandfather's family. Their house was only a few miles away, and she recalled her family's habit of packing a wagon with provisions and children to come to our house to spend three or four days visiting. Out of curiosity I asked if she remembered Uncle Gordon, of whom I had heard so little. Again, in that same soft Delta voice that my mother had, she told me:

Of course I do. Oh, honey, he was a beautiful man, but his drinking was terrible. Aunt Lula [his wife] had a terrible time with him. And when the drinking was bad, I think he saw Luther. Why, I remember the whole family. I even remember the day they brought Luther home. I was just a child standing by the front gate when they came by. A man was riding behind him with his arms around his waist holding him up in the saddle, and Luther was bleeding all over himself and the man and the horse too. Oh honey, it was a terrible sight. And it was Gordon's fault. He and Alfred were in a saloon in Red Fork drunk as Old Billy, and Luther had been sent over there to make them go home. Well, Gordon and Alfred got into an argument, and Luther, who was cold sober, stepped in to stop it and got killed. He got between them and caught the knife that was aimed at Gordon. Luther was still alive when they went by our house, but child, I knew he was a dead man.

The way this mortally wounded man was brought home is evidence of the condition of the road, which was too muddy much of the year for a wagon and team to get over it. According to the doctor's bill, also in one of the trunks, he lived almost two weeks. The doctor came to see him every day for thirteen days at five dollars a visit.

"But what happened to Alfred?" I asked Miss Hattie. "Oh, he left for a time. The judge sent word to your grandfather to get him out of the community or he would surely be prosecuted, and nobody wanted to see your family dragged through that. But he came back after a while, ruined. But cold sober. As far as I know, he never took another drink. There was not a finer man in the world than Alfred."

I tell myself that since there are barroom brawls everywhere and there are indeed muggings in the streets of every city, perhaps it is only the sense of tragedy conveyed to me as a child that leads me to believe that the South is different. But I do not believe this; the people who get killed in bars are never anybody I know, and the mugger on the street in New York would be a stranger to me. The trouble in the South is that there is a terrifying possibility that one's relatives or acquaintances will feel called upon to do violence. I was constantly warned about putting myself in a situation where it might happen. This meant anything from going to taverns or other places where people got drunk to wearing shorts on the farm where I might be seen and therefore spoken to or even looked at suggestively by any of the black men working there. If this should happen, it was implied, my father would be forced to "do something about it." What he would do in such a case was never spelled out, but it sounded terrible enough to convince me. There, in the middle of nowhere, while my friends in town were lying around in swimming suits getting tan, I could not even mow the lawn in shorts if any "hands" were working around the home place.

I wonder if the traditional southern white fear of violence at the hands of blacks is at bottom really a belief that the whites deserve it, that one night the blacks will have taken all the abuse they can stand and will simply rise as one and murder the whites in their beds. On the face of it, this is a fairly logical explanation, since the whites routinely have committed more violence on blacks than the reverse. The entire social structure from the time of slavery on has been organized for an easy assault on black people. Yet there has always been a fear among southerners of violence at the hands of blacks. Mary Boykin Chesnut describes such fear in her *Civil War Diary*, and it was prevalent in the Delta when I was growing up. None of the incidents of violence that I can recall from that time involved assault of any kind by blacks on whites, yet I too spent a terrified night once, waiting to be murdered in my bed by a black man. I expected violence that I thought had been promised and did not doubt would come.

It is important to remember that people who live out in the country, far from law enforcement officers and without telephones, are responsible for protecting their own. No matter what came to our door, it was my father's responsibility to take care of it; it was up to him to decide what had to be done and then to do it. Late, late one night I was awakened by persistent knocking on the door, and finally I heard Daddy get up to go see who it was. A black child's voice that I recognized as belonging to one of the children on the place said, I thought, "Oh, Mr. Boss, Daddy's got a gun and's about to kill y'all." I heard my father reply that it was two in the morning and dark as pitch and he couldn't do a thing about it until daylight. I lay there in a cold sweat for hours waiting to be shot. I remember that there was a mouse in the room that night whose rustlings in the curtain sounded exactly like someone trying to step in through the window. I must have drifted off to sleep, because the sun was up when I woke, still alive. Everybody else was already up and talking about it; my father was home again from looking into the problem. One of the men on the place had gotten drunk and threatened to shoot his wife and children. The child had said, "Daddy's got a gun and's about to kill *us-all*," not "you-all," as I had thought I heard. In retrospect, and this is evidence of my acculturation to violence, the most frightening thing to me was not hearing the right noises of reassurance. I would have been comforted by hearing the action of my father's pump gun or the click of shells sliding into the chamber of his double-barrel twelve-gauge shotgun. If I had heard those noises, I might well have gone right on back to sleep, confident that my world was safe for another night at least. If I could expect the threat of violence, I expected to be protected from it by violent means.

I would not presume to describe the terror of the black children who came to the door that night. Maya Angelou, who lived right across the bottom of the state at Stamps at the same time, has done it very well in *I Know Why the Caged Bird Sings*. As I said in the beginning, all I am trying to do is trace *my* pattern in the tapestry that depicts the southern experience; my fear and expectation of violence are part of it.

I believe that this kind of thing—lying in bed waiting to be murdered and doubly terrified because the comforting click of a shell being pumped into the barrel of a shotgun is lacking—has an effect on the developing consciousness of a child. It gives a peculiar cast to dreams and nightmares and literary visions. Southerners simply have different nightmares, as they have different ideas of heroism. For example, several years ago, I woke in tears from what I realized, even in the middle of the night, to be an archetypal southern nightmare. If I had to put my finger on the one most telling difference between me and Americans from other parts of this country, this dream would be the key. I do not believe that I would have had it if I had grown up on a farm in Minnesota, or New Hampshire, or Wyoming. In it, Bob and I were adults, sitting on the porch of that farmhouse, which was, strangely, still unscreened. The screens were put on about 1942, so the porch in my dreams was my memory of the way it was before I was eleven, although I myself was grown. As we sat there, a young black woman came hurrying down the road, which is about thirty yards from the house on (at that time) the other side of an orchard. A young white man was hurrying along just behind her. She turned into the hayfield across the road and began to run. So did the man. She wove back and forth, and so did he, as if they were playing some kind of game, dancing a pattern in the cut-over field. And soon there was another man, then three, and I realized they were chasing the woman and she was trying to get away from them. Then there were dozens of men after her. Although there was such a crowd I could no longer see what they were doing, I knew they had caught the woman and killed her. By that time the orchard and front yard were filled with men. I stepped off the porch to see who they were and found that some of them were the grown-up little boys I had gone to elementary school with in Watson and had not seen since I had been sent to Dumas to school in seventh grade, after the second schoolhouse burned. I called them by name and tried to shame them for what they had done, but they laughed at me as though nothing I could say would matter. I started into the house to call the sheriff, but my brother put his hand on my arm and asked if I thought I ought to get involved. After all, I had children to consider. And suddenly my older son, in the dream a child of ten or so, came out the front door and said, "Mama, make the call." I woke in a pit of grief and despair equaled in intensity only a few times in my life. I think that the grief came from knowing that my unconscious was right and furthermore, that not only in the darkness of dreams, but in the broad daylight of reality some of the boys I knew as a child, as grown men, might be the stuff that mobs are made of. And that my own brother might be unable to take a dangerous stand in a righteous cause, and finally, that I would be expected to participate by silence in outrages that I knew to be wrong. The elements of the dream that connect it with my childhood indicate a consciousness of guilt present in me all my life, recognition and acceptance of which put me at odds with the prevailing culture. Otherwise, why were the murderers people I knew but had not seen since childhood? And why did I grieve? The only hopeful thing about it was the suggestion that my son would be different from my generation.

Another element of this dream interests me. In it I almost commit the most heroic act a southern white can perform, and that is to take a risk, preferably of one's own life, to save a black from lynching. It is probably a mark of my own feeling of moral inadequacy that I did not dream myself a true hero, but an observer who objected in a helpless manner to the wrongdoing. Racism has set the parameters for a brand of heroism nurtured only in the South, and the southern white consciousness has produced a literary vision to exploit it. The theme runs through modern southern fiction, from novels like Ellen Glasgow's *The Voice of the People* through Faulkner's *Intruder in the Dust* to novels that came out of the Civil Rights Movement of the 1960s, such as James Whitehead's *Joiner* and Madison Jones' *A Cry of Absence*. One is left to wonder how often these heroic acts were performed in real life. My unconscious answered a question for me in this nightmare that I have pondered: What would *I* have done in a situation requiring me to risk myself and my family and take on all that goes with such a commitment, to save a black person? Surely it is significant that I woke up before I even called the sheriff, an act that in this case would have been after the fact anyway.

5

White and Black

As I have already mentioned, I was once seated next to Allen Tate at a dinner party in Minneapolis; after exchanging credentials, Mr. Tate and I fell into a conversation southerners in the North frequently have, about the problems of exile. This must have been about 1965, when the burden of dealing with Nothern Liberals was heavier than usual. According to their vision, each and every southerner is responsible for everything that has ever happened and ever will be happening at any given moment in the South, a notion to which I also generally subscribe, as I am sure Mr. Tate did, since he was not a man to shirk his responsibilities. But the context in which we were expected to defend ourselves in those days had its ironies. For example, the thing that interested us that evening was the fact that we saw so few blacks in the North and were surrounded by them one way or another in the South. "Why, I'm nevah invited to dinnah with any black people," he said, peering around the larger dinner table. "I don't even know any at the university. Now I know I probably wouldn't be invited with any in the South either but from the way everybody around here talks, you'd expect things to be different in this part of the country. At least down home you'd *see* them." And of course you did. Everywhere. (And nowhere.) We lived in a sea of black people whose positions were as fixed in our minds and imaginations as the sun, moon, and stars. It took a while, but eventually I understood that part of the northerners' inability to grasp the complexity of life in the South came from their ignorance of the omnipresence of blacks. Since segregation was not so much an attempt at *apartheid* as an effort to prescribe the paths of communication between the races, these paths were open to a variety of possibilities within certain limits. In small towns, there were black people living among whites; cooks and their families often lived in the backyards of the houses where they worked, and the line between white and black residential areas was often no more than a street. In Dumas, for example, the black side of town, with its own schools and churches, bordered the area where the richest white families lived. In Watson, which was considerably smaller, literally everybody knew everybody else, black and white. (If truth were told, there were more frequent paths of communication than people wanted to recognize. The census rolls for 1880 still categorized people as "white," "black," or "mulatto," and there was an interesting number of mulattoes listed in Desha County. Since there are few secrets in country villages, surely the parentage of those children of mixed race was known to all.)

But the most common path of communication was through black women who worked in white households. Around every white household I knew anything about, there were black women in some capacity or other, at least one day a week. They were privy to most family secrets, and the whites were privy to some of theirs. As for our situation, the six or seven black families sharecropping on the place added up to some sixty people. Because there were few white children within walking distance that I was allowed to visit during most of my childhood, if I played with anyone at all most days, it had to be the black children of the women who worked around the house for us.

One such black child, a girl named Little Frankie, and I spent a whole summer catching crawfish in the swamp and pulling them apart to get the tiny blue disc they have between head and torso. According to Little Frankie, these "blue plates" would bring us luck. To catch crawfish you don't use a hook, you simply tie a piece of fat pork on the end of a line and drop it to the bottom. When a pincer grabs it you feel a tug and give the pole a jerk that sends the creature flying over your head to fall on the bank behind you. That summer they were biting so well that we couldn't stop to pick them up as we flung them back there. We would wait until the bank was alive with frantic bodies trying to hustle back to the water before we started slinging them into our bucket to be dismembered later, just before time for Little Frankie to go home. We caught so many crawfish that by the end of the summer we had a water-bucket half full of blue plates, each about half the size of a dime, and the only good luck I could see they had brought us was the continued incredible luck we had at catching crawfish. We caught so many that I became obsessed. In my nightmares, giant crawfish came creeping into the house, over the floor, onto my bed. When I was awake, I was sure that the dark under the bed was really a huge crawfish waiting for a hand or foot to hang over the edge. I would leap into the bed from several feet away to save myself. I became so certain that there would be one in the drinking water every time I raised a glass to my mouth that for the last few weeks of that summer I drank nothing but milk. School started and ended this spell. Little Frankie, of course, went to the black school, and our paths never crossed again; they moved away after the cotton was picked that year. Still searching for that elusive luck, I look for a blue plate in every lobster I eat, so far to no avail. I remember that her mother, Big Frankie, taught my mother to iron a shirt like a professional, a trick she had picked up in a prison laundry.

Since some of the black families had been there as long as mine – had come, in fact, as slaves belonging to my great-grandfather – they felt free to comment on us, and the ease with which my brothers tanned was interesting to them. "Mr Jobie, how much darker is you going to get?" asked Elsie one day, "You already dark as Cuddin Annie." Her cousin, not his. There was one ancient woman from across the swamp named Aunt Kate who was allowed certain liberties because of her age and status: she was the only one still around who had been born in slavery. She would wander all over our house talking to herself and looking into things; once it was discovered that she had spit snuff juice in one of Jodie's new tennis shoes. It was excused because she was the one who did it, and the alternative had been spitting on the floor. My mother hated these visits but would not stop them because of an unspoken feeling that Aunt Kate had rights.

And then there was Victoria, whose name was pronounced "Victoerie." How can I tell about her? Most things in the South are complicated, but perhaps the hardest to sort out is the business of the black woman in the white kitchen. Actually, Victoria wasn't in the kitchen, but all over the house; she set up her ironing board wherever there was a cool breeze, out of the line of traffic. But first she washed, and that took all day on the back porch, scrubbing clothes on a rub board with water heated in an iron pot over an open fire. There was just enough room left on the bench with the two wash tubs for me to sit. Ironing took a day or two because everything had to be starched stiff as a board, even the khakis my father and brothers wore. And when I was not in school, I was wherever Victoria was, talking and listening. I consider her one of the primary influences on my life. She shaped me as surely as my family did, in many crucial ways undoing their damage. For one thing, while the men and boys in the family were agreeing with all white society except my mother that I could not do whatever I wanted to do, because I was a girl, Victoria was agreeing with me that, yes, indeed, I was going to do and be whatever. My ambitions changed weekly, but the basic aim to go somewhere and do something, to see the world and try it all out, remained constant. And no matter how farfetched my plans were, Victoria's responses were always positive, ranging from "Sho" to "You sholy is" and "You gon' show 'em, honey" or just an appreciative grunt. It did not matter that such affirmations came from one with no power at all – from someone, in fact, to whom my dreams must have seemed even loonier than they did to my brothers; they were still affirmations, and it strengthened my sense of self to know that somebody else in the world besides my mother and me thought that I could do what I wanted to. (We turned out to be right and the men wrong. I have done most of the things that I wanted to do then, with the minor difference that I took a Ph.D. rather than an M.D. and have not graced the operatic stage. Yet.)

And what did Victoria and I talk about? Everything. My plans, her family, fishing, the world situation including the war in Europe and Hitler, religion, whatever. Most days we worried some about what she could find to fix for supper. "Long as I got three things on the plate," she would say, "it be all right." Later, when I had to face house-wifery, I recognized the symmetry in having three things on a plate. I shudder when I think of the problems she had in scratching to-gether enough for that family to eat when the garden season was over.

But the complexities of our relationship transcended the chitchat we had about whether I would be a doctor or an opera star or whether Victoria would cook sweet potatoes or black-eyed peas for supper. I am curious about the effect it had on me to spend so much time with a woman who treated me with respect I got from no-one else and who let me in on the intricacies of a world so different from ours that the stories she told me are among the few glimpses I have ever had of it. For hers was a world suspended on a slender thread over chaos I could barely imagine, even when told about it in graphic detail. In addition to the usual penalties exacted from her for being black, Victoria had to cope with a husband who drank and gambled and generally was a disgrace to her very respectable family. He could not even be depended on to show up when she borrowed our ice cream freezer and fixed a big Sunday dinner for her mama and brothers and sisters and their families. He was probably still drunk somewhere in a ditch, she reported sadly to me one Monday after such a fiasco. My father continually threatened to send Jim away for good but was prevented by loyalty. Jim, after all, was descended from slaves on the place. But in spite of his "trifling ways," there was never any doubt that Victoria loved Jim, and on at least one occasion he owed his life to the fact that she loved him too much to cut his throat, which she had planned and prepared to do.

It happened this way. One summer Jim started running around with a bad influence, a man named Fats. They had, according to Victoria, been "carryin on" so indiscreetly that everybody in the com-munity knew about it. They were a disgrace, and Victoria was find-

ing it harder and harder to look her mama in the face. Jim was coming home only for the occasional meal and change of clothes; he was
sleeping everywhere else. Things went along, and one afternoon Fats'
wife Georgia came to see Victoria and pointed out to her that their
low-down husbands were making fools of them before God and
everybody and that they didn't have to put up with it. No sirree, nobody said they had to be laughed at. "Let's us," she said, "take our
butcher knives to the singing tonight at the church and slit their
throats from ear to ear." Victoria was grieving so badly that she must
have been out of her mind, she told me later, because she agreed
to do it and sharpened her knife up like a razor.

They got to the church after the singing started and waited outside
for the intermission when everybody would come out to cool off.
Sure enough, there came Jim and Fats down those church steps
laughing and joking and having the time of their lives flirting with
the girls. Georgia stepped up and stuck her butcher knife right through
Fats' throat. Victoria said she looked at Jim and understood for the
first time what she was about to do. It had been very well to *talk*
about doing it, but when the time came and she got a good look
at him standing there with a grin on his face, she thought, "Lord,
I can't stick Jim. I *loves* him," and turned around and started home.
When she had gone fifty yards or so, she looked around and saw
Georgia coming after her waving the bloody knife she had pulled
out of Fats' neck after she cut him. It was a bright night, and Victoria
could see that Georgia was coming in a hurry. Sane now, herself, she
thought that Georgia must have been as crazy as a tick to murder
her husband like that and was surely on her way to catch up with
Victoria and kill her too, for not holding up her end of the bargain.
So Victoria began to run. When she looked back Georgia was running also, waving the knife and yelling something that Victoria did
not wait to hear. She ran as fast as she could, but no matter how
much speed she put on, there was Georgia pounding along behind
her. Victoria told herself that maybe Georgia wasn't really chasing
her but just running down the road toward home. To test this, she

rolled under a barbed wire fence and started across a cotton field. Along came Georgia under the fence and across the field too. No doubt about it, Victoria saw that she was being chased by a murderer with a bloody knife in her hand. On they went. Finally, when Victoria reached her house, so out of breath she could hardly stand up, she found the door locked tight on the inside. When she banged on it, Jim hollered out that he was in there and would *never* open up. It turned out that he had seen the knife in her hand and started running about the same time she had, and the shortcut he took got him home ahead of her. By the time Victoria had banged on the door a few times, Georgia was leaning on the gate trying to get her breath back. Between such a rock and a hard place, Victoria jumped off the end of the porch and ran another quarter-mile to a house where some people took her in and let her spend the night.

This all happened on a Saturday night, and I had already heard about it, of course, by the time Victoria got to our house to wash on Monday. But her account, which I have given here, was much more interesting than the tale that had come from Jim through my father to me. Victoria said that by Sunday night it was all over, as far as she was concerned; she and Jim had made up, and he had sworn "never to step out again if she would just promise not to use no more knives."

The effect of such tales of passion, told by the woman involved, on a child from a world as passionless and pale as my family's was probably incalculable. So few hints of passion were allowed in our family that to this day the notion of sexual intercourse between my parents, in spite of the six children they had to show for it, is inconceivable to me. The only conversation I ever had with my mother about "that sort of thing" happened when I was sixteen or so and amounted to her telling me that you could always tell a nice girl because she couldn't stand to be kissed on the neck. Nobody ever said, in our house, that sex was dirty or distasteful; it was simply too awful to be mentioned at all. And yet I knew very well, on some level, what Victoria meant when she said that Jim was "carryin on," and that it was serious enough to make her want to kill him.

By Monday, she was no longer the least bit upset by the whole thing. By then it was just an interesting item, and she had begun to see the humor in having thought that Georgia was after her with the knife. The logic had come to her on Sunday: since they had arrived together, it followed that they should leave together, so when Victoria took off, Georgia did too. Everybody was so busy trying to keep Fats from strangling on his own blood that nobody tried to stop Georgia when she left. That's all there was to it.

Fats did not survive. On that Sunday the sheriff came for Georgia, and she eventually was tried and sentenced to life imprisonment for second-degree murder. (The matter of degree was probably determined by the absence of whites in the matter. Murder among blacks was not taken seriously by the judicial system.) Years later, home from college and spending the day talking to Victoria while she ironed, I asked whatever happened to Georgia. "Oh, you ain't heard about that, then," she said, and told me the end of the story. Georgia had died in the insane asylum in Little Rock. This is the way they discovered she was insane. At that time it was possible for responsible citizens to parole prisoners to work around their homes. Prisoners in for murder were thought to be the best for this, because it was unlikely that they would steal. (And, indeed, when Jimmy Carter went to the White House, what did he do but send home for a newly-paroled murderer as nurse for little Amy!) So the sheriff paroled Georgia to cook for his family. One night they had a big dinner party planned, with lots of guests invited, and when the time came, Georgia called them to the table and filled their water glasses, and it turned out that was all she had fixed. She had not cooked a thing, and they found that she did not even know who she was anymore and what she was supposed to be doing, so she had to be committed.

All of my life I have enjoyed good talk more than anything, and the talk with Victoria was so consistently good that I am sure I learned to appreciate a particular kind of conversation by talking with her, and that is the conversation one carries on while doing something else. It is somewhat like the exchange of confidences between prisoners or passengers on a ship. You know you are going to be together for a short time only, and during that time there is a sweet trusting that compels clarity and completion in spite of distractions. I remember once holding up the edge of a rug so that Victoria could sweep dirt under it. She did not signal for me to do this, but I could see that if I didn't, the dirt would have to go on top of it. The transaction did not interrupt the flow of our conversation.

But there were other incalculable effects of this black presence, for there were troubles to reconcile. I learned early the shame of betrayals in which I played a part, but for which I was not responsible. When noon came, I would be called to set the table in the dining room for the family; my friend had to wait until we had finished and then eat in the kitchen. This arrangement made me cringe and yet it was beyond my imagination to think of her at the table with us. We were in transparent spheres like bubbles that passed into one another and then out again; but we could not get out of our individual bubbles, no matter how, in certain situations, they might combine. So absolute was the separation of other aspects of our existence, and so limiting to the imagination, that one of the biggest shocks I got in a time of surprises, my first week up north in graduate school, was seeing blacks playing golf. And yet I have no doubt that I went to graduate school to study English because an exceptional high-school English teacher named Dorothy Few, in class one day during my sophomore year, ventured the hypothesis that blacks might be as competent as whites if they had a chance to prove it. I was fourteen years old, and that was the first time I had ever heard an adult make that statement. I thought so, too, and so did a few other students in that class, but the Delta in 1946 was hardly the place for a white schoolteacher to survive making statements like that, and indeed she lasted only one more year there. But the spark had caught; that teacher touched a nerve that had never been touched before, and I wanted to be like her, the first liberal I had ever laid

eyes on. If she had been the algebra teacher, I would probably be
a mathematician today. Because I was deeply bothered by the whole
race question, ashamed and terrified at the same time. How could
I be certain that my elders were wrong when they predicted the end
of the world with the end of segregation? *And yet I knew that they
were wrong.*

My greatest source of childhood guilt was the whiteness that put
me on the side of those who believed in the system and had the
authority to keep it going–people like my father, the preacher, the
governor, the senators from my state and the states around it, the
school superintendent and teachers, the policemen, judges, and all
the doctors and lawyers I had ever heard of. Everybody with any
power seemed to believe that things should be kept the way they
were. And one of the ways things were lay in the power whites had
over blacks in practically every aspect of life except religion. Under
the plantation system, this included the power of life and death,
because doctors would not treat black sharecroppers without a note
from the landowner guaranteeing that the bill would be paid. Once
a child on our place got a fishhook in his ear on a day when there
was nobody in our family at home. Treatment was refused at the
emergency room at the hospital in Dumas until the distraught mother
went to the drugstore and got a note from the owner, who was
known to lend money and also knew my father. But in this connection, the most searing memory I have concerns the terrible argument I had with my father when Victoria had one of her babies. Jim
came and said the doctor said to tell my father that the baby must
be put into an incubator at once or it would die, so would he sign
a note guaranteeing the bill. No, Daddy said, he couldn't see his way
clear to doing such a thing for all the usual reasons: wrong time of
year, the crop looked slim, etc. When I accused him of being a mon-
ster, he looked at me with genuine hurt and said, "Why, honey, I
never even heard of putting a nigra baby in an incubator." There were
things that white people did not think of in terms of black people,
and expensive medical care was one of them. Somehow they took

the baby eighty miles away to Little Rock, where the university hospital had a charity ward. I must have been about thirteen at the time. *Life* was just then publishing the photographs of the German concentration camps, and so it must have been about then that I began to understand fascism and to identify my father's generation as Nazis, a habit I have never been able to break and one that makes Sylvia Plath's poem "Daddy" especially poignant for me. I was interested, when *Sophie's Choice* came out, to see that William Styron makes his protagonist Stingo face this connection between his own experience as a southerner and fascism. The incident about the incubator changed things between my father and me; I never stopped loving him, but I never saw him in quite the same way after that.

People have asked me why I was different from others around me on this question, and I do not have an answer. I do not know that I *was*. Perhaps everyone felt as I did when young, and then got hardened into the old patterns by forces that they could not control but that I simply left behind when I went away to college at seventeen. I don't know. But I do know this: it has become the fashion to doubt that there were genuine ties of affection between some blacks and whites in the South. But in fact there were such ties, and it is a tribute to the human spirit that it could be so. The heart finds ways to accommodate and get what it needs.

There was another black woman in the neighborhood who was always close to my family. Her name was Aunt Sing, and she and Uncle John owned forty acres joining one of our fields. (I would like to remark here on the custom white people had of using "Aunt" as a title of respect for older black women. Custom dictated that they not be called "Mrs.," and white people with no breeding always addressed all black people by their first names. But "nice" white people, those with "raising," used the honorific "Aunt." It is worth noting that blacks themselves use a different pronunciation. They say "Ahnt," probably, I suspect, to distinguish the word from white usage.) It was at Aunt Sing's house that my father left the things that Santa Claus was going to bring, so that we would be surprised on Christmas morning; he always went back to her house on Christmas Day with a box of fruit and candy as a present. During the war, when we were short of sugar, she made us a cake each Christmas with her own ration. I would stop to chat with Aunt Sing when I rode my horse by there, and she always wanted to know what everybody in the family was up to, how my mama was feeling, and so on. As I rode away, she would call to me, "Now, honey, don't you ride next to no tall corn, you hear?" This was warning against the drunken, sex-crazed rapist thought to be lurking everywhere. But I knew that my brother Jodie was Aunt Sing's favorite. She was partial to him because she had saved his life and so considered him hers. One day when he was three or four years old, she looked up to see a wagon tearing down the road, driven by a drunken farmhand who probably did not even know that the child was standing dangerously near the back of the wagon. One jolt, according to the way she told it, and he would have been a dead baby. So she rushed out, stopped the team, dressed down the driver, and took the child home. This was her story; if those mules had been going as fast as she said they were, she would not have been able to get out there fast enough to stop them. But from then on, she was interested in Jodie's every move. She required frequent reports on his whereabouts during the war, and by the time he got home from the army, she had begun to consider her mortality and what to do with her property when the Call came. "Go get Mr. Joby," she said one afternoon to her step-daughters, "I ain't going to leave this property to a bunch of no-count niggers like y'all." So Jodie was fetched and informed that she had decided to leave her forty acres to him, so would he please just get the papers fixed up so she could make her mark and get things settled. He thanked her, of course, but declined. She had no choice; he explained, he would love to have the farm, but by rights it must go to Uncle John's children. (She never had any of her own.) One of those children lives there still, over a hundred years old now, and says that the first thing she does every morning is look over "at the big house to see what's stirring."

I don't know how they saw us; I am sure their feelings were as mixed about us as ours were about them. They had reason to hate us as well as to love us, and I think that our family was not as bad to them as some might have been. Everything I have read on the subject written since 1960 leads me to believe that they did hate us. And I remember once, when I was very small, playing with a little black girl who kept stamping her foot on the ground in our back-yard and insisting, "This right here where the *devil* live; Mama say so." I kept trying to argue with her and set her straight; that was not where hell was, it was much deeper and somewhere else altogether. But I never forgot the incident and years later realized that she very well may have been quoting her mother, who was talking about my father. And yet I cannot entirely believe that they all hated us. They must have made exceptions, as we did. When there were noises in the night and I lay trembling in bed waiting for the Negroes who were said to be going to cut my throat some night, it certainly was not Victoria or Jim whom I expected. And I think that talking to me probably entertained Victoria as much as it did me. Those were long, hot summers so slow it was hard to tell even that the earth was rotating, so much was one day like every other, and we helped one another pass the time. One night, many years after I had left the farm for good, Victoria and Jim picked up and took the bus to Chicago, without, as my sister said somewhat bitterly, so much as a fare-thee-well.

The last time I spoke with Victoria was on the telephone from the Chicago airport in 1966, when I happened to be passing through. I remember the day well, because something else interesting happened on it, too. At that time, I was about to finish my Ph.D. at the University of Minnesota and had decided to visit friends at Purdue and the University of Illinois on my way down to the farm at spring break. I was taking my two little boys south for the first time since getting divorced and was toying with the idea of looking for a job at a southern university so that I could raise them close to my roots. However, since I thought it might be prudent to look at a couple of midwestern university towns before making such a decision, we flew to Chicago, where I rented a car, and then drove to Urbana and Lafayette and on back to the Chicago airport to drop the car and continue on to Little Rock. We got back to the Chicago airport on a filthy, snowy day and were met at the rental car drop point by a huge, surly black man who communicated only in grunts until my six-year-old told him where we were going to visit relatives. At this he whirled around to me with a dazzling smile. "I bet y'all goin' home, ain't you?" he said, as he grabbed the bags out of my hands to take them into the terminal for me. "Now y'all enjoy your trip," he said to the boys and hurried away. For him, too, "home" was still somewhere down there, as it was for me, in spite of everything. When I called Victoria that day, she cried out in genuine surprise and, I swear, pleasure: "Why, Miss Margaret, how you *is?*"

I don't know what to do with all this. Victoria still lives up north, just now in Nebraska. I hear about her from time to time through her son-in-law, who still lives in Dumas. My father died thirty-three years ago, when I was twenty-six years old. I cannot recall the sound of his voice, and I am no longer sure what he looked like. It is a hard thing to say, but if seeing him were possible, I doubt that I would recognize him. I have not seen Victoria either, since the day we buried my father, when she and Jim were standing by the gate as we came out of the cemetery. But I would know her anywhere I met her. Anywhere at all.

6

Friends and Neighbors

I have always thought that Faulkner and Chekhov must be the consummate provincial writers, because their provinces are everybody's province. They are certainly mine. My family, with its dual father and mother figures and its brooding over Civil War injustices that seemed more immediate than the German invasion of Poland, might well have been in Yoknapatawpha County. And there was something so Chekhovian about our situation that I have always recognized his characters the minute they emerged from the wings. Aunt Sally and Grover, my oldest brother, giving up their own youth to take care of family, could have stepped right out of a Chekhov play. And our family's oldest friends, the Irbys, take their places on this provincial stage along with us. The doctor, standing alone in the center of the stage in *Uncle Vanya* and musing on getting more and more peculiar from being bottled up in the nowhere of backwoods Russia, reminds me of Stephen Irby, the head of that family.

There was certainly something old-fashioned and Chekhovian in the formality of the relations between my parents and the Irby parents. The Irby place was some three miles from ours, and, although my father and Stephen Irby had grown up together, they called each other "Mr. Irby" and "Mr. Jones." Mrs. Irby was probably the closest friend my mother ever had; she was certainly the only one whom Mother visited in the way housewives do. They would take the children and spend the day with each other sewing, canning, or just chatting. My mother was terribly fond of her, yet they too addressed each other as "Mrs. Irby" and "Mrs. Jones." There was an Irby child

The Cheshire family at nearby Red Fork, about 1896. Gordon Jones stands apart at right.

to match every one of us, and, until we were six and his mother died and things fell apart for them, Dan Irby and I were inseparable.

Their household was different from ours; there was less semblance of order in it. I have mentioned that adults in my house did not ride herd on the children; but our house looked like a prison compared to the Irbys'. We at least were expected to sleep in the house in our beds; on hot nights, the Irby children would go to sleep in the trees if they felt like it. Pauline was there on occasion and did it with them. Their house was in a grove of ancient oak trees with fat branches close to the ground, branches with forks convenient for a small child to curl up in. Once when Jodie was spending the night there, one of the Irby children gave up his bed for him and slept in the bathtub. They did exactly as they pleased. We ate with our feet under the table after a decent blessing; the Irby kids ate when and wherever it caught their fancy. I remember picnics among the roots of those giant trees, that the four-year-old Dan and I had boiled the eggs for. I also remember the odor in that house, the odor of every German farmhouse I have ever been in, that comes from milk standing to turn sour for making cheese. (The Irbys took milk seriously enough to own a cream separator, otherwise unheard of around there.) Mrs. Irby came from the community of German rice farmers across the Arkansas River, people my father scorned for their thrifty ways. He claimed they would go into a saloon and order a drink of whiskey "right up to the top" while holding thumb and index finger around the rim of the shot glass to make it taller. "Those Germans across the river" were considered passing strange, and everything they did was worthy of comment. Whenever we needed something we could not afford, Daddy would say, "Well, we'll just have to do like the folks across the river." He meant we would do without; they did without, according to him, even when they could afford not to, so stingy were they. (In flush times, he had his suits and even his shoes made to order. I remember a man coming from Memphis to take his measurements.) There were tales of the peculiarities of Mrs. Irby's family, blown all out of proportion, no doubt, by the local penchant for storytelling. For example, it was told that once, when some new ground was being cleared, her sister Pearl Lou was standing nearby when a live rattlesnake was thrown on a fire of burning brush. Talk led to her being dared to touch the snake. Before the stunned observers knew what was happening, she had grabbed it by the tail, popped its head off and taken a bite out of the still writhing body.

My father disapproved of the Irbys' household, and especially of the way they raised their daughters. Roberta, the one who matched my sister Pauline, was constantly held up to me as a cautionary example; her shameful behavior consisted of riding their pony Bonnybird bareback. Young ladies did not ride bareback. To illustrate the outrageous extent of her conduct, at the slightest excuse Daddy would tell of the day he was riding his horse across the bayou bridge when he heard the thunder of hooves and somebody yelling like an Indian. It was Roberta, *riding bareback and sitting backwards* on Bonnybird, shrieking "Hello, Mr. Jones" as she tore down one bank, through the shallow stream, up the other side and on out of sight. (All the kids knew that Bonnybird hated the bridge.) Roberta was probably all of fourteen at the time, and Daddy thought that this kind of behavior could lead to no good. He probably thought it was the first step down the road toward being a loose woman. The effect the story produced in me was envy: I wouldn't have tried it backwards; I might run our horses until they dropped, but I always faced forward. Contrary to Daddy's expectations, Roberta grew up to be a model of respectability.

Dan and I played all kinds of games together. We made ink out of pokeberry juice and drew pictures with it, an enterprise made interesting by warnings to be careful; pokeberry juice is deadly poison. We played endlessly in barns, yards, our swamp, and their slough. But, best of all, we played store. Store was best because there was a real one to play in. For years Mr. Irby had run a flourishing country store because he loved to talk. But neighborhood gossip had it that Mrs. Irby decided that it was wasteful for him to spend all of his time waiting for customers, so they installed a bell in front of the store that the customers were supposed to ring to summon somebody from the house to wait on them. This was alien to the spirit of a country store, where people do more visiting than buying and certainly want to spend their money where they are welcome to sit down and talk. Within a very short time, there were no longer any customers, and the store with its remaining merchandise and equipment sat there waiting to be violated by children. There was a cash register, an adding machine, and even a typewriter. It was cool and dark in there and smelled of linseed oil and decay; there was a thick coat of dust over everything, and there was something the tiniest bit frightening about it, as if there were presences there we could not see. I remember the delicious knot of fear and expectation in my stomach when we crawled in through the window that the children all knew was not really nailed shut. The door was supposed to be locked; I doubt that it was. We would have gone in through the window anyway, under the circumstances, because of the added thrill.

Mother thought that Mrs. Irby's insistence that Mr. Irby stop minding the store which he loved, and be a fulltime farmer, which he hated, was as tragic in its way as her premature death, for it started an acceleration of his peculiarities that snowballed in a very short time. Mr. Irby loved the *idea* of business. He loved keeping books in the same destructive way a drunkard loves his booze. As long as he had the store, he had an active set of books to keep and work he enjoyed; deprived of these, according to local myth, he became obsessed with two things: keeping a balanced set of theoretical books and pondering the unfairness of the government's decision to run a drainage ditch across his property. He retreated into himself and spent more and more time "working on his books," as he said. After Mrs. Irby's death, the light in his office would burn until the early hours of the morning, and everyone who passed by would say that he was up there struggling with accounts, as his land bit by bit slipped away from him. He never had been a particularly attentive farmer, and as the problems he thought up for his accounting increasingly took possession of his mind, more and more he let the farming go.

His other obsession, the drainage ditch, led him to rave about the "infernal revenue service" that exacted drainage taxes to support a ditch he did not want. He wanted to lead a movement to stop people paying taxes to a government that could step in and put a canal across a man's land without his consent. He was almost violent on the subject and so alienated everyone – including my father, who began to dread meeting him. Mr. Irby could not understand why such an old friend as Daddy would not join him in his protests. Perhaps the fact that the ditch was not on his land entered into his assessment, but my father looked on the drainage ditch as salvation. It was part of a system of canals that, coupled with improved levees, was designed to avert another disaster like the 1927 Flood.

But before Mrs. Irby died, when Dan and I were six, that household had a joy that ours lacked. The contrast has come to be symbolized in my mind by the differences between our orchards. Theirs had trees laden with soft, luscious freestone peaches that melted on the tongue. Ours had tight, firm-fleshed clingstone fruit that had to be chewed. From the things I have told about my house, I think that one might get the idea that we were happy. I do not think we were. Something oppressive took the joy out of everything, and the likely culprit, in my opinion, was religion. The Irbys were not religious in the same way my family was, Mrs. Irby having come from a family of Christian Scientists; and I suspect that therein lay the differences in the families' attitudes toward life. I place a lot of blame for our solemnity on the Methodist Church.

If the Irbys were Chekhovian, our next-door neighbors, the Duttons, were more Faulknerian in style. Generally speaking, around our house God was God, but Franklin Roosevelt ranked somewhere up there close to Him. However, one mistake the Roosevelt administration needed to be forgiven for was buying the Duttons a farm through the Farm Security Agency. And the farm it bought for them was the one that my father's sister, Aunt Maggie, had let slip through her fingers years before, her patrimony that lay right next to our land and had our graveyard on it. Occasionally the question would arise in our house of what could be done if the Duttons ever got ornery enough to shut the gate and refuse us entry to our own graveyard. At least Bob and I worried about this possibility; the adults probably weren't concerned about it, since they knew that, on a day-to-day basis, the Duttons needed our goodwill more than we needed a cemetery. Because they borrowed anything in the world they needed from us and never paid it back. Daddy liked to tell about the time somebody gave them enough catfish for a fish fry and they invited everybody they knew and then sent to our house to borrow a sack of meal and ten pounds of lard to fry them with. Mother said she could not refuse to send whatever Mrs. Dutton asked for in the middle of cooking a meal because she could not bear the thought that the children over there might go hungry. I remember once when a child was sent to borrow coffee and Mother looked in the canister and saw that we were almost out too. "I can't let you have coffee to-day, honey," she said. "Look here in this can, this is all we've got and it's barely enough for breakfast." The child looked mournfully into the can and replied, "But we ain't got none."

We did not visit with the Duttons, but we knew them well. The men, three generations of them, hung around our machine shop where the farm implements were repaired whenever there was work going on in it. They were such fine storytellers, according to all the males in our family, that they were always welcome, Furthermore, their domestic affairs were conducted at the top of their voices, and occasionally we were drawn into them.

I remember one winter evening we were sitting in front of the fire reading and listening to the radio, when we heard a terrible commotion coming across the pasture. It was the two older Dutton girls screaming, "Help, help, Mr. Jones, Grandpa's killed Daddy." My father and Grover rushed across the pasture to the Dutton house, where they found one man unconscious but coming to in response to a great deal of cold water that had been thrown on his head. He had been hit by his father with a singletree, which is a piece of harness made of an oak stick about three feet long and three inches thick, with iron on each end. Father and son had gotten into a heated discussion about something, words had led to fists, and then the father had picked up the closest weapon at hand and knocked his son, aged about fifty, in the head with it. As soon as Jim, the son, recovered, Daddy and Grover came home to tell the tale to the rest of us. No sooner had they gotten settled, however, than there was a knock at the door. The old man had come to explain. He was clearly embarrassed and deeply shaken, because he had thought at first that he had surely killed his son. It was the only time I ever saw any of the adults from that family in our house. I recall how strange it was to see him sitting there, all hunched over, in an overstuffed chair. With his long white hair and flowing beard, he looked like Father Time. It was told of him that once in a fight he had bitten off a piece of the inside of his cheek that remained attached as a sort of flap in his mouth that he chewed on when agitated. He was certainly chewing on it that night. "Yes," he said reflectively, staring into the fire, "I guess I just tapped him a little too hard."

The Duttons had parties that we could hear very well all the way across our orchard and their pasture. Somebody would play a steel guitar for dancing, and often, about midnight, when the urge to eat would hit the revellers, we would hear the chickens squawking as they were grabbed off the roost and slaughtered for the skillet. At our house such Dionysian carrying-on was thought scandalous but funny.

Before the government bought them that farm, the Duttons, or Mr. Dutton and Miss Cook, as they were then, had been tenants on our place, and Daddy had insisted on their getting married although they apparently had lived successfully in sin for years. There were several older children of previous liaisons around the house, and they had had one daughter together who was some three years younger than I. Frances Dalilah Jean, whose name was shortened to Punky shortly after her birth, was underfoot at our house for a few years, following me around and worrying me to death. When I was totally bored with everything else, I would be reduced to actually playing with Punky, who was too young to hold any interest whatever for me. She it was who played chicken with me in the matter of seeing who could let the snakes come closest to our bare feet. The only advantage to her company was that she would do anything I told her to without hesitation. We could play together anywhere on our place and anywhere *outside* on theirs, including the beautiful Roosevelt barn, which was better built than most of the dwellings in Desha County, but I was strictly forbidden to go *into* the house over there. But of course I did. Whatever my family feared would happen there before my innocent eyes never occurred. My lasting impressions of the place are of a general mess, with Punky's mother in a shapeless print dress, feet bare, and lip full of snuff, cooking dinner, while the old white-bearded grandfather, coughing terribly with asthma, shooed chickens out of the kitchen with his cane and complained bitterly that, since people left the screen door open, were it not for him the chickens would get on the table and peck the food right off their plates. They would, he said, end up eating chicken tracks. The only thing I recall ever eating over there were tea cakes half an inch thick. Ours were thin.

The opinion in our house was that the Duttons were poor because they were shiftless, not because they did not work. They worked very hard and were good farmers, but whatever money they had as each bale of cotton was sold would be drunk up or lost in a crap game on the way home from the gin. Eventually they gave up being landowners and went back to East Texas, whence they had come. Before they left, the older daughters drifted from one kind of trouble to another and then away. I remember when one of them, about eighteen years old at the time, left to hitchhike to Chicago. As she stood by the road with her suitcase, waiting for the first ride of her journey, Mr. Dutton stepped out on their porch and shouted this last piece of fatherly advice: "Now, Ruby, you cut tem corners, y'hear?"

When I was a small child, for a few years I did have one true friend within walking distance of our house, and, although I was not allowed to go to her house to play, she could come to mine. She was the daughter of a farmer whose land lay at the back edge of ours. According to my mother, he had had a "nice" wife, who died before I started first grade at the age of five and met Rosetta, who was bright, bright, bright. We were close for three years; I was not to find such a compatible friend again for many more. It was well known in the community that her father could not write, and Rosetta told me of trying to teach him to write his name and read after she had learned how in the first grade. She was unable to teach him more than to sign his name. I was a sturdy child and larger than Rosetta, although a year younger. The summer before we were to enter fourth grade, Rosetta's father, worried that something had stopped her growth because she was not keeping pace with my size, took her to a doctor who decided there was some malfunction in her thyroid gland. He prescribed powerful medicine to be taken something like *once* a day for a week, then discontinued for a week, then resumed for another week. Rosetta duly read the instructions on the bottle to her father, who insisted that he had understood the doctor to say the dosage should be three times a day until the medicine was used up. He later told how he would not listen and she had been right. The powerful dosage sent her into convulsions and then a coma from which she did not rouse for weeks; when she did, she was completely mindless. She sat staring for the rest of her life and died in the state mental hospital when I was fourteen.

I remember after forty-five years the day my father came in in the middle of the afternoon to tell me that Rosetta was very ill and had been taken to the hospital. I was expecting her that afternoon; she had been at our house two days before. The news about her got worse and worse, but I could not understand that she would not be all right. I was taken to see her once after they brought her home from the hospital. She was lying in a bed in white pajamas with pink flowers on them; somebody handed her a piece of wrapped candy and she turned it and turned it in her hands, not knowing what it was or what to do with it. Once shown, she could not even put it in her mouth.

7

Moderate Brimstone

It is necessary to understand that religion is different in the South than in most other places; there it is as pervasive and persistent as the heat and humidity of summer. Evidence of its centrality in the southern imagination can be seen in the fact that differences between denominations that may seem academic elsewhere are of vital importance there (all Protestants, I am told, look alike to Catholics and agnostics). One sees what one is trained to see, and the training in spotting religious differences starts early. One of the first stories I remember about my grandfather on Mother's side, a Methodist circuit rider, concerned his ability to *smell* a Baptist as far as he could see him. I myself, by inclination as a-religious as I could possibly be, can identify a Baptist playing the piano by a peculiar set of runs set into the arrangement of their hymns. Once Baptists learn to play those hymns, they throw the runs into everything. Van Cliburn *looks* so much like a Baptist that the first time I heard him play, I was surprised to find that he left the runs out. The jokes considered funniest in my family were about doctrinal differences between Methodists and Baptists, especially the need to immerse the Baptists totally during baptism because the few splashes considered adequate for Methodists would not do the job on their wickedness. It was told that Grandpa Cason, the preacher, once had a congregation of Methodists that was split right down the middle by some doctrinal difference that caused such violent feelings that he had to put a loaded pistol on his pulpit to keep the members from fighting while he preached. I am told that people in the hills where I live now occasionally still come to blows in the yards of country churches over what they consider misinterpretation of Scripture.

The question of why southerners are burdened or, as many believe, blessed with a sharper sense of sin and knowledge of evil than other Americans, is certainly worth pondering. Put another way, why did the religious fervor that landed with the first settlers in the South not dissipate, as it did in New England, but become distilled into something stronger? Isolation, ignorance, and poverty no doubt contributed as much to this aspect of southern culture, as they do to all the others. The teachings of the Bible loomed larger where there were few distractions of any kind and virtually no intellectual currents that would encourage fresh philosophical thought. But while all the answers continue to beg the question, it is certainly true that the powerlessness of people like mine in the face of the elements that controlled both our lives and our livelihood nourished the need for the comfort of a divine hand. There was no buffer between us and the arbitrary behavior of nature. People are dependent on the authority directly above them; those who work for corporations, the government, or even the local store have a structure between them and the weather's devastation of crops. They may ultimately suffer if the cotton crop fails or the river washes everything away, but the connection between the disaster and their lives is blunted. For us there was no such structure. There was no mitigating factor. And so a faith as simple and absolute as my mother's could mean the difference between living in constant fear and despair, as my father did, or in serenity and hope, as she did. I remember his complaining once because, after a long drought which almost burned up the cotton crop, we had so much rain that water was still standing in the furrows when the hot sun came out, and he was sure that the tender plants would be scalded before the hands got water furrows going to drain the fields. Mother, serene as ever, ran her eyes over the flooded fields and said firmly, "I'm *sure* God has something in mind."

There are advantages for English teachers in this background of religious teaching in the South. I find it easier to teach *Faust*, for example, to students here who seem personally acquainted with the devil than it was to students in Minnesota. And they find Flannery O'Connor's novella *The Violent Bear It Away* believable, because in every class I have ever taught it to, at least one person had known of a local prophet.

The subject of religion is tied up with a lot of other things in my life that have always separated me from my family in spirit. Now that we are older, my youngest brother Bob and I seem to be leaving behind some of the differences that have always existed between us, the indefinite, not quite definable barrier, that has separated us from the beginning. They have always said, in the family, that I was "different" from birth, but they have never been able to put a finger exactly on what that difference consists of. Whether a matter of heart or mind, it manifested itself early as an inability to believe much of what I was told, while my brothers and sister seemed eager to embrace it all. For example, they were willing to accept the joyless vision of a Methodist world in which anything that brought pleasure was suspect, while I was not.

I am certain that the southern Founding Fathers hit on that religious negation of pleasure as a counterweight to the prevailing sensuous atmosphere, because they feared a culture given up to the voluptuousness that was natural in such a climate. The mixture, on that heavy air, of the scents of magnolia, honeysuckle, wisteria, and a strange musk exuded by the armyworms as they ate the new cotton blossoms gave such an erotic tone to summer nights that a strong opposing force had to be exerted to keep us from a life abandoned to pleasure. In fact, some settlers in that very vicinity had not handled it as well as we did. Thomas Nuttall, writing of his travels on the Arkansas River in 1819, described the French at Arkansas Post, the oldest settlement in the United States west of the Mississippi and a bare ten miles from our farm, as being dedicated solely to fine clothes, parties, and dancing. He was appalled at their refusal to concern themselves with mundane affairs, even the cultivation of kitchen gardens, despite the abundant slave labor they had to work them with. The result, as any good Methodist in my family could have predicted, was ruin. They lost both land and caste. There are still a few vaguely French names around there; in fact, the original county seat of Desha County, the one that caved into the Mississippi in 1874, was called Napoleon. But by the last years of the nineteenth century, the French at Arkansas Post had fallen on such hard times that it is told that one might come across the barefoot, ragged descendant of a chevalier of France following a plow behind a skinny mule in an isolated field carved out of swampy woods, his patch of ground the last remnant of a land patent granted to an ancestor by a grateful French government before the Louisiana Purchase. A cautionary vision like that was enough to keep the noses of people like mine to the grindstone for generations.

For ours was the faith of fathers who had come to this continent to make a garden of the wilderness in more ways than one. To keep their children pruned of idle fancies, they took us to church every Sunday morning and also every night for a week during the revival meeting in the summer. Our church was a simple little building in Watson, the town nearest to the farm, six miles away. To get to it in the summer, we had to pass several temporary brush arbors erected for revival meetings of denominations infinitely more joyful than ours: "Holiness" or "Pentecostal" sects of one brand or another whose members believed that the Holy Spirit would actually come down and enter their bodies, speaking through them in "unknown tongues." When they "got the Holy Ghost," as they called it, they would roll around on the floor moaning and jerking in an ecstasy considered by Methodists to be past all bounds of decency. The people who attended these services were mostly from the hills and not anybody we knew very well. But whatever the religious intentions or results of their meetings, it seemed as obvious to me then as it does now that they were having a much better time than the solemn members of our congregation ever had, and that my mother would never let us go to those services because she did not approve of that good time. She probably thought that, in their abandon, they were making more than a joyful noise unto the Lord. Judging by the racket to be heard for a mile in any direction from those arbors, the only good times comparable were to be had in the black churches and honky-tonks, to which, of course, we were not allowed to go, either.

In *our* church, especially during the revival meetings, we sang sad hymns designed to impress sinners with the gravity of their situations so vividly that they would repent in time, before the brink of hell on which they were standing crumbled and dropped them into the pit to burn forever. The only people who ever seemed to be having a good time were the visiting preachers, who may have felt freer to engage in histrionics before strangers than before their own congregations. The preachers probably couldn't have sustained such carrying-on on a weekly basis, and the congregations wouldn't have put up with it if they *had* been able to. Not Methodists, anyway. Our own minister was a quiet man, not given to threats, who mobilized guilt simply by looking us in the eye. He may have invited such fire eaters for the revivals to make up for his own lack of energy. The revival hymns were even worse than the ordinary run of bathos that we usually indulged in, such as "The Old Rugged Cross" and "I Come to the Garden Alone," our preacher's favorites.

I remember one visiting preacher who would begin with a quiet prayer and a peaceful hymn to provide the theme of his sermon and slowly build to an intense, lunatic rage. No matter how hot it was, this one always started in a jacket, although he was the only person in the church not provided with a fan advertising the funeral home. As he warmed up with the preaching, he would start mopping the sweat pouring down his cheeks, and finally, in a frenzy of arm-waving and raging, he would tear the jacket off and settle it carefully on his chair at the back of the podium, as if he had taken the weight of the world's sins off his own shoulders. We knew this to be the climax of the sermon because, when he turned from the chair to the audience again, he no longer exhorted, he pled. "Oh my friends," he would whisper, "can you *imagine* what it would be like to feel the flames of hell for all eternity?" Then he would request some old tearjerker like "Just As I Am, Without One Plea," designed to shame the most sedentary sinners in the house into coming to the altar for salvation. If there were no results by the time we had worked our way through all four verses and choruses, he would call to the pianist, "Let's start it again, I *know* there are those who *hear* but cannot make the decision." And we would launch into another set. And it worked. There were always results at revival meetings. We sang until there were. Two, three, sometimes as many as eight or nine would go down and either join the church or rededicate their lives to the service of God. When the two preachers agreed that nobody else was likely to be giving in that night, the newly saved were lined up and baptized on the spot, it being one of the practical marks of Methodism that very little equipment is needed for baptism. Our preacher would hold a bowl of water as they went down the row, and the visiting preacher would dip his hand in and sprinkle a little water on the head of each repentant sinner, while murmuring the baptismal formula. Then the congregation would be invited to file down and "give the hand of fellowship" to the new members, some of whom might never be seen in church again. These victims of an emotional trauma would be congratulated around town for a few days, and then everybody would seem to forget the whole thing.

Such was the case with me. During a particularly feverish service when I was about eight, I thought I heard the preacher say that anybody who had never joined the church and failed to do so that night would surely go to hell. In the face of such a choice, I did what any sensible child would have done: I marched down and joined up, which was barely all right with my family; since I had been christened as a baby, the baptizing I got that night was superfluous. They probably let it go on because putting a stop to it would have caused a stir, and they would never do anything that called attention to us. Four or five little Baptist girls sitting in the same pew followed me down and got baptized as Methodists; *their* parents would have stopped it if they had been there. They were visiting our church just for the show and, according to their parents, were taken advantage of by at least one preacher who *knew* who they were and what he was doing.

My family's attitude toward this outer sign of my salvation was interesting. They did not seem particularly pleased; I think it was because we were expected to hold ourselves and our dignity a couple of notches above the emotion let loose once a year in that congregation. We were supposed to be above it all; that is why we were christened at birth. We did not need to "join the church" to reach a state of repentance, we were already in it. If I had been sitting by my mother instead of by those little girls, she would probably have held me down with a firm hand on my knee to keep me from exhibiting myself in such a fashion in public. In my family's view, public displays of religious emotion were as bad as any other kind and, though countenanced in others for the sake of their souls, they were denied to us. Members of my family flatly refused to lead any prayers in church, even to pronounce the benediction at the end of the service. My father seemed uncomfortable even saying the blessing before meals, and some confusion in his mind about the nature of prayer may account for the slip of the tongue once when he bowed his head, cleared his throat, and began, "Please start the biscuits around –." I suspect this reticence in emotional matters was part of a larger mission, thrown up to us by Mother at every opportunity, called, "setting an example for the community."

At any rate, I felt pious for a few days, even after Bob set me straight about what the preacher had *not* said, by explaining that I had misunderstood, Methodists do not believe people go to hell if they are not baptized in the Methodist Church. And then boredom with religion set in and afflicts me to this day. But my brothers have always seemed to live in thoughtful piety. If I wanted to do something Bob knew the adults would frown on, like riding bareback or sneaking off with the twenty-two to shoot turtles on Sunday afternoon, he would look me seriously in the eye and ask if I thought God would approve of such behavior. I could not then imagine him doing anything considered wrong by anybody, and I still cannot. Three of my brothers are pillars of the Methodist Church in the communities where they ended up. They lead what appear to me joyless, teetotalling lives, taking grape juice at communion, passing the collection plate on Sundays, and casting a suspicious eye on me – doomed, they probably believe, not because I lead a particularly sinful life but because I willfully chose to be different from them in this as in other matters.

But back to my original speculation about the lessening of that difference. Bob visits me two or three times a year to continue the arguments we got in the habit of having as children. He chooses the topic on the way up, drops it on the coffee table between us when he arrives, and we settle down and go at it for hours. Whether the subject is political, social, or theological, we argue as if our lives depend on the outcome. Since our views are almost diametrically opposed on everything, I was stunned a few years ago to find that the armor he has always used as a defense against this awful world may be more a matter of what he thinks he *ought* to be than of what he might be under different circumstances. I may have misjudged him. Our differences on religious matters may not lie so much in what we believe as in the way we act on those beliefs. Because that time, when we were talking about the Cajuns in southern Louisiana, where I had just been to photograph some plantation architecture, he remarked in a voice of wonder, "You know, if I didn't have a family depending on me, no wife or children or anybody but myself to worry about, I'd like to go live with the Cajuns. Because they are just about the happiest people I have ever seen. Why, they eat well and they drink and they dance and they just *carry on* all the time." That fantasy may not sound like much unless you know what it is to be a southern Methodist like my brother, with a nose to the grindstone. What an admission to come from him! And what proof of my theory that Methodism and other brands of southern religion have served well the intentions of our forefathers to prune *us* as brutally as the forests they cleared for farms!

8

Books and Learning

When I first left the South, I found the attitude of others toward my background hard to bear. I was defensive when the off-spring of butchers from Queens or beer makers from South St. Louis were critical of the cultural milieu that had spawned me. But I soon learned not only that it is difficult for urban people to imagine the isolation in which we lived, but also that when they do grasp it, they find it hard to believe that any people at all were literate. But there were books, and people read them. There were books in our house because my great-grandfather and grandfather had bought them from itinerant book peddlers who came around in wagons, and when we had money to spare, we bought them too. The *Arkansas Gazette* also ran serial novels that everybody read. (Pauline claimed that when she was young, Mother would read the daily installment first and cut out anything she thought unfit for the eyes of an innocent girl.) The Irbys had a set of *The Book of Knowledge* that made them insufferable authorities on everything. Every one of them could stop any argument with a quotation beginning *"The Book of Knowledge* says –." Mother would read book reviews in the *Gazette* and try to get hold of books that struck her fancy. The Book-of-the-Month Club, when we were finally able to join, was a godsend.

What I would like to convey, however, is concerned with an *attitude* about books and learning that, more than anything else, fostered a desire for information and entertainment via the written word. I have already noted that our pleasure in the spoken word was indulged by constant storytelling, and that habit undoubtedly

carried over to appreciation of stories in print; people who grow up in
a storytelling tradition know a good story when they read one. But we
were fortunate to have books in our house, and we knew it. I remember
being appalled to hear my classmates tell about taking their new books
home the first day of school to be devoured word by word by their
parents, who had nothing else to read. They would also select books
from the meager school library that their parents would enjoy. Because
of the poverty and isolation that surrounds so many of them, southerners perhaps have had more occasion than others to sort out the difference between ignorance and stupidity, a distinction lost on most out-
siders. Northerners, with all the kindliness they can muster, ask me
how it happened that I, rather than the others around me, got an education; translated, that means, how did I know enough to even want
one? The best answer I can come up with is that I was lucky enough to
be born into a family that had owned some land for a long time. Certainly, when I was a child, there were many others in the same community who were capable of doing anything in the world, had they but
had an opportunity. (I have always found it ironic that so many of the
people who patronize southerners in this way are people who make
their living teaching and criticizing literature but do not always know
a good story when they read one and couldn't *tell* one if their necks depended on it.) In fact, four of the six children in my family and five of
the seven Irbys took degrees. Furthermore, mine was not an isolated
case, as the number of southerners on the faculties of midwestern
and northern universities proves; southern universities are, by and large,
staffed by people who grew up much as I did. The only difference between me and some of them is that I happened to go north to graduate
school, where I fell under the gaze of nonsoutherners, who thought I
must be atypical, as indeed I was simply because I was up there. The
true ignorance lies in the eyes of the beholders, who, most likely, have
seen so few educated southerners because they have never been in the
South. Many more southerners go north to college or university now
that there is more money, but naturally, even more stay in the South
for their education.

I attended school in Watson from first to mid-seventh grade, and I do not think I have ever been better taught. The teachers were a pleasure, and I marvel now at their dedication under such trying circumstances. They were overworked and underpaid and might as well have been living in a fishbowl. All eyes were on the teacher, and one misstep in the community's rigidly prescribed path meant immediate dismissal. But they had the respect of the community; in that place at that time, being a teacher meant something. They, in turn, took their responsibilities seriously. I enjoyed school from the first day I was allowed to go, which happened when I was barely five. The rule was that children had to be six, but since I was ready to go and my father was on the school board, no questions were asked when I was taken and enrolled on the first day of school in the autumn of 1936. School was magic to me then; it still is.

I could read before I went to school, where we studied the usual things. I recall there was lots of homework, and I enjoyed it all. I also enjoyed recess and lunchtime. There was little equipment on the playground, so our entertainment took some invention. There were seasonal pastimes like marbles for boys and jacks for girls in the spring. The girls played hopscotch with broken pieces of glass for markers, jumped rope, and "jumped the board" endlessly. For this latter, a thick plank from six to ten feet long was placed over a chunk of split firewood, and a competitor stood on each end of it. It was like a seesaw, except lower, but one on which you stood. The object was to jump so hard on your end of the board that your opponent, who would fly into the air, would miss it coming down. Advantage was given the less skilled, sort of like handicapping in a horse race, by moving the board off-center on the chunk so that one end would be longer than the other. The big girls in the seventh and eighth grades would send each other five or six feet into the air, and when the especially skilled ones were jumping board, there was always a big crowd to watch. The good ones took it very seriously and would challenge each other to a match that would determine who was best once and for all. They could keep it going for long periods of time, flying six or eight feet into the air and coming down gracefully on the board. I was never any good at this or at jumping rope, either. The jumprope went so fast that it was worth your life to "run in," which everyone over the age of five was expected to be able to do, without stopping the rope. Pauline told me not to jump the board because my insides might fall out, and I believed her, but I suspect that I refrained from doing it because I was just plain scared. It was dangerous; every now and then somebody would take a bad fall. I saw one or two split heads, but nobody was ever killed, although this was a genuine possibility.

Another spring diversion was playing along the bayou bank when the water was high. I think we threw sticks in to see how fast the current was going. I remember one whole spring that was taken up with digging out miniature cave dwellings in the clay banks of a deep ditch that went by the school grounds. Elaborate fantasies went with the caves. Unfortunately I cannot recall a one. When all else failed, we would choose up sides of twenty or so children armed with switches and simply fight over a specified area of the playground. The point was to gain control of the territory in the center of this area, and the winning side was the one able to drive the other one back to its starting line. This game was forbidden, but I recall playing it over and over. There was not much supervision on the school-ground, to say the least.

When I started school, there was no lunchroom; one was provided by the government about 1937 or 1938, I believe, serving meals made of "commodities"– that is, surplus food of all kinds that farms all over the country were producing when there was no market for them. I remember a lot of beans and canned grapefruit. Before the lunchroom arrived, we took our lunches from home and, after eating them, found some excuse to go "uptown." You couldn't go without permission, so you had to need a pencil or tablet or something else essential to be allowed to go. I remember the walk there and back better than the stores and what we went to buy. First we had to cross the bayou, at its deepest point, on a wooden footbridge like the one in the story "Billy Goat Gruff," in which a ferocious goat lurked under a bridge waiting to butt children. Then we crossed the railroad track, where there was always a freight train on the crossing at noon. Without fail. The trains took on water, cotton, and logs at Watson, so they were there a long time. Since we had a limited amount of time to get to town and back, there was no question of waiting for the train to move. The big kids climbed over it, up the ladder on one side, a crawl across the top, then down the ladder on the other side. I never did this. I crawled under it with the other little kids. To this day I remember the thrill of being nose to nose with a big iron train wheel that, for all I knew, would start turning any second.

Because of the cultural desert in which we lived, a desert without museums, libraries, bookstores, record shops, art galleries, concert halls, beautiful buildings, or anything else smacking of "high" culture, a great deal depended on the quality of instruction and leadership provided by the school. During the time that I went to elementary school in Watson, a marvelous man named Colburn Cox Stuart was superintendent of schools. Although trained as a teacher with even some postgraduate work at the University of Chicago, Mr. Stuart had come to the community to buy a farm and run a business. When the superintendent's job fell vacant, a delegation of parents asked him to take it, and he did so with imagination and energy. He was smart enough to get federal assistance so that he could pay his teachers real money instead of the warrants teachers in other districts received. (These warrants were letters of credit given against the time when a school district would have money to back them up and were accepted by local merchants and boarding houses at a discount of their already minute face value.) And he was smart enough to know the value of education. He would take promising seniors to the campuses closest to us, introduce them to the college presidents, and ask that they be given ways of working their way through. He made it desirable and possible for many to go to college who would never have done it otherwise. And he also believed in the civilizing value of literature, painting, and music. I remember vividly a traveling exhibition of pictures that he brought to the school. There were hundreds of reproductions of Old Masters hung on rows of temporary partitions, floor to ceiling, about three feet apart, all across the school auditorium and two classrooms, pictures that we would never have been able to visualize larger than the pages in a book if he had not brought them (and that he himself probably wouldn't have known about if he had not gone to graduate school in Chicago). Seeing Rembrandt that one time at the age of eight had a profound effect on me, because it showed me something out *there* to want to see again. Mr. Stuart and Mother were in league, of course, and when the schoolhouse burned down the first time, she donated our books to the school library. She said she could not bear for those children to be without any books at all. Giving them up would not deprive us, because we could check them out at school with everybody else. I remember the pick-up truck backing up to the house to haul them off. Only a few of the old books were left: a leather-bound history of the Civil War, an 1890 biographical dictionary of everyone in the county who could afford the fee for inclusion, and an 1843 publication entitled *The Male Generative Organ in Health and Disease from Infancy to Old Age.* This last was probably one of my great-grandfather's acquisitions, undoubtedly considered unsuitable for young eyes.

Music was thought important also, and Mrs. Dobson, the piano teacher, was another civilizing influence, for more reasons than the appreciation of music that she conveyed. For not only was the spring recital taken as seriously by the participants and their mothers as a prodigy's recital at Carnegie Hall, it was the social occasion of the year. I remember once running across a stage in deep preparation for the recital; several mothers were arranging flowers, others were fixing rows of chairs. And for some reason I stopped short by Mrs. Dobson and a mother in deep conversation about suitable attire for her daughter, the star of every recital for years. The mother was saying, "Now I realize that rhinestones show up better on a violinist, but do you think they would do for Emmy Lou to wear tonight?"

In addition to the *social* aspects of music lessons, we learned to play the same pieces all the other children in the country were playing and were encouraged to read relevant articles in Mrs. Dobson's copy of *Etude*. Aside from the pieces learned in piano lessons, classical music was outside the frame of reference at my house and so came to represent part of that world beyond us that I intended to discover. I think opera held particular interest for me because it was so mysterious. I listened to classical music on the radio every chance I had to wrest the box away from the rest of the family and finally, in my senior year in high school, managed to get to Little Rock for my first live performance of an opera. My mother's sister, Aunt Mary, invited me to come up and go hear *Madame Butterfly* with her. I was not disappointed; opera turned out to be almost as mysterious on the stage as it was on the radio on Saturday afternoons, but for me the whole thing was as glittering and shimmering as the stars in the sky. I was apparently the only person in our immediate vicinity of the auditorium not bothered that Cho Cho San weighed roughly two hundred pounds.

The music listened to in our house over the radio (the phonograph that went down in the Flood was not replaced until about 1945) consisted of popular music played by the big bands then in vogue, and black blues from the radio stations in Helena and across the river in Greenwood and Greenville, Mississippi. These latter songs were more sophisticated versions of those sung by the blacks in the fields chopping or picking cotton, where one lone singer would belt out a line and the whole group of as many as twenty-five or thirty would respond with the appropriate next line, or grunt in unison. The leader's line might be a simple statement like "Oh, sweet Lord, I feel so bad today," and the rest would answer, "Yeah, sweet Lord, feel so bad today." Then he or she would go on, "This old row so long can't see to the end no way." And the chorus would take that up, too. One song could go on for thirty minutes, with the leader adding in whatever felt right. It is more accurate to say that we *heard* this music than that we *listened* to it. It was in the air, but we disdained it. It did not interest us.

The tradition of Delta black blues has come to be recognized as one of the richest in America. There are annual festivals dedicated to it now in Helena, Memphis, and Greenville. The black musicians who play it are invited all over this country and western Europe to give concerts. But when I was growing up, when it was still in its most formative stage, when the field songs were feeding the creative imaginations of performer-composers who polished it into complex, intricate music for voice, guitar, harmonica, drums, wind instruments, and piano in the honky-tonks on Saturday night – at that time, whites considered this music as inferior as anything else "they" did. Most whites thought the music itself "low-down," and the dancing that went with it was considered absolutely scandalous. I am not particularly prudish, but when I saw the Howlin' Wolf do a "dirty boogie" in Club 49 in Cambridge in about 1965, I was shocked as I had not been shocked at the obligatory stripteases that end most Danish nightclub shows. I think it was not so much what Howlin' Wolf *did* that conditioned my response (although I do believe he was making a special effort to shock that lily-white audience), as it was my upbringing.

Nor had the time arrived when country-western music would be considered respectable. It was called "hillbilly" music in our house and was associated with shiftlessness. The Duttons listened to it on the radio, and the older girls sang it in that strange flat harmony that country people all over the world, including Russian peasants and Nigerian villagers, affect. Their mournful songs telling of somebody leaving or dying could come floating over the pasture at any time of the day or night. Songs like "Beyond the Sunset," "Farther Along," "God Put a Rainbow in the Cloud," "Life's Railway to Heaven," and "There Was Dust on the Bible, Dust on the Holy Word" were considered "common" in our house, not only because they used the bad grammar Mother thought a sign of the end of civilization as we knew it, but probably also because they could evoke real emotion if you let them. The point was not missed at our house that such religious sentiments should be lurking in people who had never been known to set foot in a church. Yet this was a particularly lively time in the history of country-western music also. It too was still in an early phase, beginning to have its fair share of radio time and playing a genuine part in the lives of millions of Americans, although it was not yet the stylized article that Elvis Presley could pick up and blend with black performing style to produce the worst of both worlds, as people like mine saw it. (They thought Elvis was scandalous, too, and that his performances should be censored if he couldn't be stopped altogether.) It is an irony worth recording that there we sat during my childhood, listening every Saturday night to Guy Lombardo playing "Stardust" and hanging on Glenn Miller's every note, while all around us two of the most vital strains of American music were developing at practically the speed of sound. This was music that actually *touched* the lives of people who sang it and listened to it; moreover, there were musicians on those farms all around us who, if alive today, would probably be driving Cadillacs in Nashville or making albums in Chicago, and the best thing I thought I could find to listen to on the radio on Sunday was the Longines Symphonette! How far we have to go before we get home! And yet, even as I say that, I know that my appreciation for this music is stuck on an intellectual level. I find it an interesting cultural phenomenon, but I don't really listen to it much; it doesn't touch me; it isn't *my* life they are singing about, so my face feels rubbery after the first verse. Mozart's Clarinet Quintet uplifts my spirit, Johnny Cash leaves it cold. The Modern Jazz Quartet uplifts it, too, but their music is almost as far from Delta blues as Mozart is.

The songs Mother sang as she did housework were either hymns or old songs like "Go tell Aunt Rhody the old grey goose is dead, the one that she's been saving to make a feather bed." At one time she had been able to play the guitar rather well, but by the time I came along, all she remembered how to perform was something called "The Spanish Fandango." Occasionally somebody would hand Daddy a fiddle, and he would render "Over the Waves." Pauline remembers that when the older children were small, long before I was born,

Mother would play the guitar, Daddy would fiddle, and they would all sing late into the night. I don't know whether this went by the board naturally when the radio came and they no longer *had* to make their own music, or whether sadness over such things as losing my brother Paul snuffed out the songs in them. I am sure it was the influence of the radio that nourished the interest in popular music. Pauline and Grover loved to dance, and there were enough young people around to have dances with, to the music of a wind-up Victrola. Also, there was "the boat." Once a year, an excursion boat with a dance band on it touched all the viable docks on the Mississippi River from Memphis to New Orleans, took on everybody who could dance, and floated out onto the river for five or six hours of dancing. The women wore formals, and a debutante ball could not have been more exciting. This custom had ceased by the time I was old enough to go, but I remember vividly the worry and planning that went into Pauline's dress.

The school at Watson was considered the center of the community, and most people, whether they had children in it or not, took an interest in whatever it offered. Everybody went to recitals, the plays performed by both junior and senior classes, Christmas pageants, and end-of-school extravaganzas in which every elementary schoolchild took part. The busses were sent to bring people from the country who did not have cars. People have told me of remembering their parts in these performances for years and reciting them while they did housework or worked in the fields. The comfort of cultural matters was not lost on these people; it was just the opportunity to be taught that was lacking. If that school had taught the students from first grade on that it was desirable to know about operas by teaching them to sing arias, they would have done it willingly, and their parents would have gone to hear them. But their tradition was otherwise.

It was also thought in those days that the school had a responsibility to help parents teach manners and social grace. There were too many Baptists in Watson for dancing to be allowed at school functions, but the Junior-Senior Banquet was a big occasion, at which young men and women were expected to dress up and practice good behavior. Everybody helped with the event by cooking food and serving the dinner. Mother and Miss Jones thought it tragic that the schoolhouse's burning in 1939 would deprive that year's crop of its banquet, so it was held at our house. All the furniture was taken out of our living room, dining room, and two front bedrooms, to be replaced with tables made of sawhorses and rough lumber from the shop classes. Chairs, dishes, and white tablecloths were borrowed here and there, and I remember the shine all over everything that night in May when I was allowed to stay up and watch through the kitchen door as some of the biggest louts and bullies who rode the schoolbus behaved like gentlemen.

When I was in seventh grade, the new schoolhouse, built to replace the one that had burned three years earlier, also burned to the ground one night. Although Daddy was a member of the Watson school board, he thought it best to send Bob and me, the only children in our house still in school, to finish at Dumas, twelve miles in the other direction from the farm. Dumas was a richer school district and had a good high school. My graduating class had twenty-eight people in it, but the curriculum at that tiny school was certainly adequate preparation for college. We took four years of literature and composition, three of mathematics, a year each of European and American history, a course in government, at least one year of Latin (although two were encouraged), and a year of biology. All of these courses were extremely well taught except biology, which was the purlieu of the coach. There were district academic competitions every spring, and our school always took medals in drama, extemporaneous speaking, Latin, algebra, and choir.

There were movie houses in Dumas and McGehee, and the children who were old enough to drive went to them. I did not get to go much until I could drive myself there on Sunday afternoons. The few times I was taken as a child I embarrassed Pauline and Grover so much by asking questions that they vowed never to take me *anywhere* again, ever. Miss Jones and Mother liked to go when there was something suitable. I remember their grunts of disapproval when Rhett Butler said "damn" in *Gone With The Wind*, a film that stirred patriotic sentiments in all of us except Daddy, who refused to see that or any other "talking" picture show. For some reason he took pride in never having seen one that talked. He was sure that the addition of the actors' voices could do nothing but detract and was determined not to be proved wrong by experience.

9

The Table

The food we ate and the reason why we ate it instead of other kinds mark another point at which the topographical and cultural "Deltas" intersect and distinguish us from others. Like the flatness of the land that does not seem unusual without hills for comparison, southern taste in food has to be looked at away from home to be understood. It never crossed my mind when I was growing up that our eating habits were not shared by all other Americans, if not indeed by all the civilized world. And if I was rudely disabused of this notion by my first meal in a university cafeteria in St. Louis at the age of twenty-one, I was forty years old and had lived in the North and in Europe for seventeen of them before I came to understand that the key to our unique taste probably lies in the large numbers of black people who have been in the South since the early 1600s. My ignorance, in this instance, was different and more serious than some of the other deficiencies that my northern friends liked to ascribe to the cultural deprivation suffered growing up where I did. The refusal by American scholars in both North and South to admit the influence of black culture on "southern" culture has resulted in a distortion of history and deprived all concerned of an interesting and valuable heritage. My ignorance in not knowing that what we ate was different was indeed the result of insularity. But I came to understand that I shared a higher plane of ignorance with everyone else. For nobody in North *or* South seemed to know why that difference existed. Or if they did, they weren't telling. Let me describe southern food and then explain my own epiphany on this culinary road to Damascus.

When I think about the food we ate, I think first about where we ate it and about the people around the table. As I have mentioned elsewhere, my father made the table itself out of miscellaneous pieces of wood after the Flood. The legs came from an old desk that my great-grandfather had brought to Arkansas when he first came, and the top was made of mahogany boards about eighteen inches wide nailed to a mahogany frame; these obviously had come from other pieces of furniture that the water had soaked apart. The whole thing was a big rectangular table that was always covered with a white damask cloth, possibly to hide the nails. I never saw it uncovered except for changing the cloth, until I was a grown woman and my sister, who moved out to take over the housekeeping after Mother died, had put it out in the old commissary building to make room for her own table. I was shocked at the crudeness of our table in its nudity, because, with the cloth on and nothing showing but the legs, it looked rather elegant. There were also always large white damask napkins to match the cloth. My father insisted on this. It was as important to him as grammar was to Mother, probably for the same reason. The dining room had no other furniture in it but the table and chairs. A sort of buffet and china cabinet was built into the wall with a pass-through to the kitchen, and varnished-cypress stairs went up the other wall.

As I say, the table was large and, until the war started and took the boys away, full. My father sat at the head, and the children sat down the sides, arranged in descending order by age, to the foot, where mother sat with me beside her. Mother told that in the early years, as each got big enough to eat at the table, my father placed the child beside him for a few years of lessons in manners. By the time I got there, his mind was no longer on the table manners of children; I always ate at the foot. When Miss Jones, the teacher, came to board, she sat in the place of honor, at Daddy's left, to be offered each dish first; sometimes, when there were guests, Miss Jones moved down the table, too. As almost a member of the family, she was ex-pected to give place to preachers but not to our relatives, who were the only other guests we ever had. We seldom had company at all, but when we did, the younger children waited for a second sitting.

I do not remember what we talked about at meals, but I remember very well what we ate. For breakfast we had fried ham or bacon – home-cured, of course – with eggs deep-fried in the drippings; thick fluffy biscuits, two inches tall and brown on top, that you buttered while they were still burning hot and spread with homemade preserves (my favorite was pear). The grown-ups had coffee and the children thick, dark cocoa. I remember a special breakfast one Christmas morning, when we had a turkey platter piled a foot high with fried quail that Jodie had shot the day before. It had taken him all day and a great deal of walking to do it, so he had been later getting home than was usual around our house. When a hunter who left on foot was not back by dark, it was assumed that there had been trouble. Hunters sometimes get tired and handle their weapons carelessly, or they fall and break a leg, or they bog down in a swamp or meet foul play of some kind. I remember the worry. When there was trouble in our house, everybody was silent and crept around. We did not talk about emotional matters; each of us suffered alone. We would draw into ourselves as if the possibilities were unspeakable, or as if we thought that voicing them inevitably would make them realities. But Jodie was fine and happy when he finally got home with the game pockets on his hunting coat bulging with quail. We never had quail any other way than fried crisp and brown, the way Mother fried chicken. And quail gravy was made the same way as with chicken, but browner and richer.

Both dinner, served at high noon, and supper, served roughly at dark, were big meals. For meat we most often had chicken or pork, because we raised them ourselves and cured our own pork, while beef had to be bought. The only refrigeration we had until electricity arrived came from the ice that was delivered twice a week by truck. So there was no way to keep beef fresh, while pork could be cured to last a year. We had smoked ham, shoulder, and bacon year 'round, and in late November or early December, when it was finally cold enough to kill hogs, we had fresh pork chops and ribs.

Hog-killing caused more commotion than anything else around the farm, because there was a rush to get it done and the meat cured before the weather changed. Cold snaps in the Delta cannot be depended on to hold for more than a day or two, and a year's supply of meat was at stake. So, early in the morning the backyard would fill up with people, mostly black, hired to help for the day. The first thing they did was build a roaring fire under the washpot to heat scalding water. Then they killed the hogs with a bullet to the brain, cut their throats to bleed them, scalded them in a barrel to make the hair turn loose, scraped the hair off with knives, and cut them into pieces to be smoked or salted. Everything was used by somebody on the place; the only thing left was the squeal in our ears. The hogs always knew something was afoot when people went out to pen them up at daybreak, and started squealing in fear. It was hard to listen to. The fattest parts were rendered for lard in the washpot, and the cracklings, the dried pieces of pork from which the hot fat had been drained, were reserved for crackling bread or to be eaten as a snack. Crackling bread is cornbread cooked with cracklings stirred up in the batter. Souse, or head cheese, was made of the heads, and sausage of the leaner parts not choice enough to be eaten any other way. My father was so particular about the seasoning of his sausage that he did it himself, the only gesture toward food preparation I ever saw him make. And he only did that, he said, because nobody would even *try* to understand exactly how much pepper and sage to use. The entrails were taken home by the blacks for chitterlings. Occasionally one of them, who knew that Daddy liked it once a year, would bring him back a mess of prepared chitterlings, and he would eat it alone while everybody else at the table ate other things; he was the only one who would touch "chitlins." On the day after hog-killing, we would have fresh sausage and eggs scrambled with hog brains for breakfast. The squeals would still be in my ears, but the sausage was marvelous.

Although it would seem that their closeness to animals would make farm families vegetarian, it seldom does, probably because few farm animals are pets. I do recall our getting so attached to a Christmas goose once that it could not be slaughtered and lived for several years until, ironically, a fox killed it on the front lawn. I don't recall ever being called upon to eat a pet pig; Bob loved his 4-H hogs, but they were sold to be eaten by somebody else. However, it is true that, although Mother loved baby chickens and would sit on a stool in the chickenyard and talk to them while they ate, when they reached adolescence and the time came to fry them up, she would wring their necks like cracking a whip. Every day she would run her eyes over the flock and pick the ones that were ready for the pan. As a child I loved to cut up the birds because I was interested in seeing the heart, liver, gizzard, and lungs, and was fascinated by the prodigality of unlaid eggs in the pullets and hens. When the war came along, I started a little egg business and sold a case of twenty dozen a week because we had the facilities for keeping all those hens and nobody left to eat either them or the eggs. It was highly profitable; the price of eggs went, I believe, to twenty cents a dozen by 1943. There was a demand for them to supply the families of the soldiers who were guards at the Rohwer Relocation Center for Japanese, situated about ten miles from the farm. (The presence of that facility is one of the many reasons that I do not believe the German claims of ignorance about the concentration camps. If this one had had a wall twenty feet high around it, everybody in the county would still have known what was going on in there.) We always had dark hens, Rhode Island Reds or Plymouth Rocks, because we liked brown eggs rather than white ones (and I was probably not the only one who thought Leghorns looked too much like cranes to eat).

When those range-fed birds, killed at the precise moment of achieving flavor but before getting tough, reached the table, they set the standard by which fried chicken should be judged. There are two schools of thought in the South about the way to fry chicken. The one prescribing heavy batter, which has been taken up by the fast-food business with such success, is not ours. Our school believes that if the batter becomes the important consideration, there must be something lacking in the flavor of the bird. Piece by piece our fryers were rolled in flour seasoned with salt and pepper, then fried in a deep iron skillet full of melted lard. That is all. It came out light and crisp and cooked evenly to the bone and was meant to be eaten with the fingers, which did not get unreasonably greasy because, without batter to hold it, there was not a great deal of grease left on the meat. When the chicken was all fried, the grease was poured off except for a few spoonfuls, flour was browned in the pan and milk or water added to make gravy for the potatoes or rice that went with it. Gravy was sometimes put on the biscuits, too, but never on fried chicken. Furthermore, we never had gravy without meat; the only people who did, did it because there was no meat, so it is with amusement that I see "biscuits and gravy" on menus today, even in the South where people know better. That kind of gravy, made without the passage of meat through the skillet first, is essentially paste, or *white sauce* as others euphemistically call it, and in our household was considered fit only for thickening soup.

When the surviving fryers reached maturity, we had them roasted with cornbread stuffing; the ones who made it to tough old age were stewed with dumplings or boiled for chicken salad. We also kept turkeys and geese and had them at Thanksgiving and Christmas. There were ducks in the yard, too, but we cared less for them. Guineas there were not; Daddy hated them because of their constant murmur and giggle.

There was game, also. Occasionally my father would go off and shoot a wild turkey, a matter of great pride by that time, because, as the woods disappeared, the turkeys got scarcer and wiser. He made his own turkey callers by whittling a little cedar box, left hollow on one side, across which he scraped a carefully whittled cedar stick to duplicate the sound of turkeys gobbling. He was good enough at it to fool hundreds of turkeys in his lifetime, and recalled that, as a boy, he could shoot them from the back steps of the house. The flavor of these birds was stronger than that of yard turkeys, and they were tough beyond belief, athletes one and all. In the late fall we sometimes had squirrels stewed with dumplings. Mother would cook them, but only without their heads. However, I remember once eating fried squirrel at Aunt Maggie's and being fascinated not only that they still had their heads on, but also that she would crack the heads with the handle of her knife to pick out the brains. Bob and Jodie were duck hunters, and I have mentioned the quail that Jodie shot. Daddy was an inveterate quail hunter also, and in season there was game about once a week. He no longer hunted deer by the time I came along, but other hunters would share their kill with us, to his delight and the despair of everybody else. Venison requires more in the way of preparation than Mother was willing to grant, so she would cook it like beef, which left the meat almost too gamey and tough to choke down. The last time I had it was the day I was married. In that empty, silent house, grieving because of Mother's recent death, with nobody there except my distraught father, my fiance, and me, I had to go into the kitchen and cook venison for the only time in my life. Daddy had saved it for me because *he* enjoyed it so much. I had had the good sense, at least, to read a cookbook and marinate it overnight in vinegar with oil and onions. I remember vaguely that even then it was barely fit to eat, but since we had a not-particularly-popular wedding to get through and a train to catch, nobody paid much attention. The thought of handing his daughter over to a Yankee was enough in itself to choke my father and take his mind off the stringiness of the venison. (In fact, when we arrived at the church and met the rest of the family for the ceremony, he declined to give me away until the preacher talked him into it.)

We had fish occasionally, whenever the fishermen in the family caught some. They were bass fishermen but would stoop to catching bream and crappie when they were biting. When we had catfish, it was bought from one of the commercial fishermen on the river, usually. Mother rolled them all in cornmeal and deep-fried them. We did not eat crawfish. Lord knows they were plentiful and were the same variety as those eaten by the millions in southern Louisiana, but it was not our tradition.

Ham – baked, boiled, or fried – was the mainstay of our table. If it was fried, we had red-eye gravy with it; pork chops were served with thick gravy. Beef was special, and tough, so we had it pot-roasted or pounded tender and then chicken-fried in deep fat. With the meat we had mashed Irish potatoes, little whole new ones boiled, in season, or shoestrings fried crisp. I cannot imagine the outrage a soggy piece of fried potato put in front of my father would have caused. An alternative to Irish potatoes was a mountain of boiled rice; served frequently also, sometimes even with rice but never with Irish potatoes, would be sweet potatoes baked, candied, or mashed. On special occasions they would be boiled, mashed, and then baked with marshmallows on top.

The meat and potatoes would be placed in front of Daddy, and ranged down the sides of the table would be large dishes of vege-tables that themselves might have made the center of a meal. Cooked separately for hours, each with a piece of fat pork, were field peas ("cow peas" they are called up north, but among us they are carefully dif-ferentiated by their individual names, such as "purple-hull," "crowder," and "black-eyed"), mustard or turnip greens, butter beans, and string beans. These vegetables had not been overcooked; each pea still stood alone. In season we had boiled corn on the cob – called, for some strange reason, "roasting ears"– or, for a change, corn sliced off the cob and creamed. We had cole slaw but never cooked cabbage that I remember, sliced tomatoes, spring onions, cucumbers, and bell peppers as side dishes. Sometimes there was sliced okra rolled in corn meal and fried. There was "pepper sauce," made of hot pep-pers marinated in vinegar, to go on the greens.

Our daily bread was made from batter, not yeast dough: either cornbread, baked in an iron skillet so it would be brown all over, or biscuits. But occasionally Mother would make "light bread" with yeast, both large loaves and tall rolls from the same dough. We had our own butter, of course, shaped in a rectangular one-pound mold. The boys milked the cows, and the women and girls took care of the milk. I hated churning but loved to mold the butter.

There was a fine orchard, so for dessert in season we had peach and green apple cobblers and pies with light, crisp, flaky crusts shortened with lard. In late summer, when Arkansas apples get ripe, we had them baked with cinnamon and sugar. On Sundays we had ice cream made of boiled custard and turned in a hand freezer. Frequently this ice cream had mashed fresh peaches frozen in it. (When I was small, it was my job to sit on the freezer, which was packed and padded with tow sacks to keep the cold in, to hold it down while my brothers turned the crank.) We also had sweet-potato pie, which is much like pumpkin pie, but sweeter; chocolate, lemon, and coconut meringue pies; banana pudding; and pecan pie made with white syrup and called Karo Nut Pie. Sometimes there was rich lemon cream pie made with Eagle Brand Milk and graham-cracker crusts. Instead of pie we might have three-layer chocolate cakes with fudge icing or golden cakes with boiled white icing and/or coconut sprinkled on top and sides. Or we might have an angel food cake that stood eight inches tall when removed from its tube pan. To appreciate Mother's accomplishments in the kitchen, it is essential to understand that until about 1946, when butane gas became available, this cooking was done on a wood-burning range without a thermostat. The cook had to know her stove incredibly well to keep an angel food cake from falling, in an oven whose temperature could be controlled only by adjusting the amount of wood in the firebox. And Mother felt inadequate as a cook in comparison with my father's sisters. Now, *there* were cooks, everybody said. I remember going to visit at Aunt Maggie's house on Sunday afternoons, when we would be offered a huge piece of many-layered devil's food cake on a plate with a dill pickle. Mixing the sweet and sour of cake and pickle would raise the hair on the back of my neck and make my tongue seem to stand straight up. Aunt Maggie's fruitcake was a triumph, too; she made it in the early fall and kept it in a cloth soaked in bourbon until time to cut it at Christmas, when of course somebody always joked about throwing away the cake and eating the rag. Everyone thought that Aunt Sally and Aunt Maggie were such good

cooks because they had been taught by the black cook the family
had had during their girlhood. And then, when Mother married into
the family, Aunt Sally taught her to cook what my father liked. In
fact, Aunt Sally was still doing a great deal of the cooking at our
house until her death during my fifth year. There was still a black
cook there when Mother arrived, but when the cook died, she was
never replaced, since Mother, who had not grown up with a black
cook in her house, could not get used to the idea of having one.

In summer the vegetables were fresh from our own garden. In
winter they came out of quart and half-gallon mason jars that Mother
had put them up in. For, in addition to the daily preparation of those
gigantic meals, during the summer she was also continually canning.
I did not really understand until she was gone that she probably
hated cooking and did it only because it was her responsibility.
When the boys went off to war, she refined her technique to the
point where cooking for my father and me took very little time. She
would keep a batch of dough in the refrigerator and pinch off a few
biscuits thirty minutes before noon and, while they were cooking,
fry up some ham, heat up a jar of applesauce, and slice a couple
of tomatoes. Daddy was even routinely fed leftovers, for the first time
in his life. She was not interested in food and resented anything that
took her from her reading. If she was still stretched out reading at
11:32, Daddy would start pacing around with his watch in his hand,
muttering that dinner was going to be late. In her opinion, there was
no longer anything to hurry for.

As I mentioned earlier, it was a revelation to find, when I first
went north, that what we ate was not what everybody else in this
country eats, because southerners, no matter where they were on
the social ladder, ate pretty much as we did. The ingredients were
the same, although the preparation might differ with the level of
affluence. In the matter of cornbread, for example, very poor people
made it with only cornmeal, water, and salt; those who had them
put in eggs and milk; anybody really putting on the dog made a
yeast cornbread loaf. Everybody ate the vegetables we ate, cooked

the way Mother cooked them. I lived in Minnesota for years and was continually surprised that, although corn grows up to the eaves of the farmhouses and thousands of acres of field peas are raised every year as cattle feed, cornbread is not a staple but an occasional treat, and nobody would be caught dead eating a "cow pea." I think it is fair to say that if students in University of Minnesota dormitories were fed what they would get at any southern university, they would quit school.

I did not begin to understand the source of this difference in taste until 1970, when an African in London served me a "native" meal that consisted of sweet potatoes; corn on the cob; black-eyed peas that he called Congo Peas; sliced tomatoes, bell peppers, and little spring onions served together on a dish; cornbread; and deep-fried goat (goat, because chicken was too expensive). A meal we might have had any day on the farm, except for the goat. And eating it made me as homesick for the Delta as it made the African for his home. Eating this food that I would not have been served anywhere in America except in the South had the same effect on me that seeing a molecule might have on a theoretical physicist. In a flash, a number of old things became clear to me, and new questions were opened. Why did I have to wait until I was forty and learn this lesson for myself? Why was I not taught in school that the elements of south-ern cuisine that distinguish it from other American regional cooking are African in origin? Even maize and sweet potatoes that originated on this continent and were eaten by Indians probably retained their popularity in the South because of the presence of large numbers of people who came to this continent with an established taste for them. For the Portuguese traders took these things to Africa, where they became popular 150 years before the height of the slave trade. Surely it is significant that when the newly-arrived slave sat down to his calabash of greens, pork, and pot liquor sopped up with a hoe cake, with a roasted sweet potato on the side, he was the only immigrant to this continent *eating his native food*. All the early im-migrants, except those in the South, learned to use maize from the

Indians and gave it up as soon as they could get the wheat and barley
growing to satisfy tastes they had brought with them. The use of
maize swept along on the cutting edge of the frontier all the way
across the country and was relinquished as a staple after the frontier
passed on, *everywhere except in the South and certain parts of the
Southwest, where it can be explained by the strong Native American and
Spanish-American influence.* In the research my epiphany drove me
to, I found that even the southern habit of deep-frying everything
can probably be laid to the Africans, who used palm oil in Africa
where we use lard over here. It stands to reason that people who
do not have ovens and cook over an open fire would not only deep-
fry but boil several items in one pot, like peas and meat.

The way all this came to be is so obvious that I am surprised at
not having seen it before I did, and it was fortunate for me that my
interest in the effects of the black presence on "southern" culture
came after the awakening of interest in Afro-American culture in the
1960s, for I was helped in my search by such books as Eugene
Genovese's *Roll, Jordan, Roll: The World the Slaves Made.* From this
and other sources, I have pieced together an idea of the way things
must have happened. Africans, from the beginning invited into the
"big house" to cook for whites, cooked what they knew how to cook
and what they were used to, ingredients that grew as well in the
South as they had grown in Africa. The plantation owners, the ar-
biters of southern taste, adapted to black taste because that is what
came out of their kitchens. If they had maintained a tradition of European cuisine by importing European cooks, African taste might not
have dominated southern cooking to the extent that it did. But even
in Louisiana, where the strongest effort was made to preserve European tradition, African cooks made Louisiana food a very different
kind of French cuisine from that in France. The question naturally
arises why southern poor whites who did not have black cooks ate
essentially the same food as those who did. I can think of two reasons that provide at least part of the answer. In the first place, the
ingredients were available, growing as readily as in Africa, and good.

In the second place, it was easy to combine "black" taste with whatever else people brought with them to make a "southern" cuisine. There is an analogy for this in South Texas, where everybody, both Hispanic and Anglo, eats chile. They even have a name, "Tex-Mex," for the particular style of cooking that has evolved from combining Anglo and Hispanic traditions, as we have a name for our cooking, "southern."

After sorting all this out, I felt betrayed by my heritage. I think that Americans have been able to discount the contribution and influence of Africans because endemic racism allowed them to. Nobody wanted to believe that blacks had any influence on whites, because the former were supposed to be inferior. We did not see it, because we were allowed not to. I do not for one minute believe that, if the slaves had been Chinese with the same access to white kitchens that the blacks had, I would have grown up eating greens and hamhocks, black-eyed peas, sweet potatoes, okra, cornbread, and deep-fried chicken.

It is worth noting that, although I remember this food with such relish and write so lovingly of it, I do not cook particularly well in this style. I was not interested in learning to cook as a child and was never called upon to cook more than a few emergency meals before I left for college. Then I married a northerner and learned to cook to suit his taste. He would have preferred a live rattlesnake to black-eyed peas cooked all morning with a hunk of fatback and wanted his chicken fried, if fried it had to be, in just enought vegetable oil to cover the bottom of the skillet. Since he would have relished a boiled rubber boot with enough Bernaise sauce on it, that is the style in which I learned to run my kitchen. But make no mistake, when I am offered southern food I fall upon it.

10

The Afterglow of the Confederacy

So far has the South moved since my childhood toward incorporation in America, that my sons find it incredible that the Civil War was such a topic of interest around our house when I was growing up. The fact that it was may illustrate the nature of defeat in a romantic cause, especially when the cause has been disputed so close to home. It certainly explains why the landscape of my mind has a battlefield in it, a fact that is not true of my peers from other parts of this country. And that battlefield, with all it implies, is one of the components of my sensibility hardest to come to terms with, one that had to be dealt with before I could come home again. For "the War" is another one of those points of intersection of the Delta of the imagination and the land as it really lies. There were no battles in our immediate vicinity, but there was a large cannonball in the yard, probably shot several miles away during the battle for Arkansas Post and hauled home as a curiosity by some hunter who found it in the woods near the river. There were also a couple of flintlock guns standing around the house that might have been, but were not, used in the conflict, and there were endless tales about the bestial nature of the Union soldiers who came through the neighborhood stealing food and livestock. This evidence of the war's reality gave it a quality that nourished our imagination. The cannonball, even though Mother had painted it silver to blend it into the border of a flower bed, could still be dodged in childish fantasies of heroism. Our own family stories about the war were added to those of everybody else we knew to build a collection that both horrified and fascinated us. The story of the Union soldiers' breaking into the Coopwood's smokehouse and stealing every scrap of meat except for one ham that Mrs. Coopwood fell on in the yard and hid under her skirts might as well have been our own. My brother-in-law Bill's great-grandfather and great-uncle had been called to the door late one night by soldiers and never seen again. Anytime we cared to, we could conjure up a Yankee patrol at the gate; there was no doubt in our minds that the enemy was contemptible. Final causes are not the stuff of childhood fantasies, and we were not taught anything in school that detracted from the notion that our side had been heroic – defeated indeed, but heroic – and our history lessons were so vague on the subject that I was not to understand exactly what had happened at Fort Sumter until I went north to graduate school. The attitude around our house seemed to be that the South was the victim of a conflict that had been thrust upon it. "They" had simply picked on us past the point of tolerance, war followed, and we had been paying for defeat ever since; witness the fact that freight rates were lower for shipping manufactured goods south than for shipping cotton north. The impression was that we were still, in 1936, under the heel of the conqueror, who, if permitted, would step in and subvert the very fabric of our social institutions. That is why we had politicians whose job it was to keep this from happening, to preserve the status quo at any cost, men whose careers depended upon their being willing to fight change by any means necessary.

But the most pressing reason for the war's overwhelming immediacy in our consciousness lay in the circumstance that Daddy's own father had fought as a soldier in the First Arkansas Regiment of Volunteers and saturated his children with the war stories he had had ample opportunity to gather, having fought in virtually every major battle of the Army of Tennessee and then walked home from North Carolina after the surrender. His stories, passed down through my father, were either generalized, having to do with the nature of war and large battles, or detailed, bloody, and graphic. For example, when a minie ball at Shiloh left one of our grandfather's fingers hanging on a piece of skin, he simply laid it on a rail fence, cut it off with his pocketknife, and went on fighting. He was in a tight spot and had no choice. His company had been attached to the Army of Northern Virginia during its first year of service, and he had witnessed the Battle of Bull Run from a nearby hill, waiting to be thrown in. In a memoir of his war years, written in old age, he remembered the cavalry charge there as the grandest he ever saw. That memoir of his was kept with other relics tucked in the family Bible, the ceremonial Bible, that is, that was never read but was reserved for keeping records of important events. Since Grandpa was a private at the beginning of the war and a corporal after four years of service (although when the federal government sent us a tombstone for him in about 1934, he had been promoted to sergeant), the glamour that accrued to his ventures in the war did not come from his position. It was not a glorious career that gave us pride, it was the fact that he had served in a glorious cause. Nobody could deny that it had been lost, but everyone we knew considered that it had been worth fighting for. As a child I could think of nothing I would rather have done than fight in that war. It had an iron grip on our imaginations. We children were hung on the hook of that great "what if"—the Confederacy had won the war. This "if" was the starting point of numerous speculations around our house, and the consensus was that the family certainly would have been better off. We would not be as poor as we were, obviously, because we would not have lost the land and assets exacted from us by the war and Reconstruction. Of course nobody took these absurd speculations seriously; surely nobody within my memory could have considered seriously the prospect of a country separate from the United States of America. Or could they? Children's fantasies are woven of the threads of myth floating around their heads.

And here the problem gets more tangled, because ultimately, when one played the game of "what if," the question of slavery had to be addressed. And this is where the shameful part comes in. Because some of the most expensive "assets" lost through the war were the slaves, and most seemed to feel that, if Lincoln had been willing to pay for them and then set them free, the war could have been avoided. It mattered not a whit that the wealth we thought we had lost had depended on slavery, possibly because the plight of black share-croppers was not considered to be much better than that of slaves with benevolent masters. Our family, it was reasoned, must have been kind to its slaves, because they did not leave when they were freed; their descendants were still right there on the place where they had always been. But it is more likely that the slaveholding in our past was not considered shameful because the prevailing climate of opinion did not allow black people the level of humanity that whites were assumed to have. I never heard my father refer to slavery in any other than a joking manner. The last slave purchased by my great-grandfather had cost eighteen hundred dollars, and Daddy would laugh and say that there were one or two people on the place at the moment worth considerably less. If anyone had pointed out the monstrosity of this joke to him, I suspect that he would have count-ered by saying that of course there were some who would be worth considerably more. Such was the nature of racism, even in a Chris-tian household that gave what money it could afford to support the Methodist Missionary Society for the conversion of foreign hea-thens! Mother would say on every possible occasion that slavery had been a terrible thing, and she emphatically did not enter into the "what if" game. But apparently it had been all right with her to name Bob after Robert E. Lee. And if she thought it was funny that Daddy preferred iron-gray horses because they looked like Lee's horse Trav-eller, she certainly never said so. Racism permeated every aspect of our lives, from Little Black Sambo and the bungling black child, Epaminondus, in the first stories read to us, to the warning that drinking coffee before the age of sixteen would turn us black. It was part of the air everyone breathed.

And so much did the world I grew up in seem in some ways like a separate country that I have never quite known what to do with myself on the Fourth of July, which we did not celebrate. At least we did not observe it the way people do in other parts of the country. You could not even buy fireworks in July; we had them at Christmas. There were no parades, either, although sometimes there was a political picnic in Dumas or McGehee. For some reason Daddy thought eating catfish on the Fourth was appropriate and would arrange to get a big one for dinner, but that was all. People worked in the fields as usual. Furthermore, I do not recall much in the way of flag waving and patriotic celebrations at school until the onset of World War II. I do not recall saying the Pledge of Allegiance, for example, before Pearl Harbor.

Ours were not the only imaginations fired by thoughts of the Confederacy, and *Gone with the Wind* fanned the flames. Just about everybody read the book and then waited expectantly to see the film. I remember a sermon by our preacher on Scarlett O'Hara's spirit, which he thought carried a lesson for us all: "When she stood on that scorched earth, barren as far as the eye could see, and raised that sweet potato to heaven and said, 'With Gawd as my witness, I'll never be hungry again,' oh, brothers and sisters, I thought to myself, there's the indomitable spirit of mankind that rests on the strength of the Lord." At the time I was interested in his graphic evocation of the scene, because I remembered it, too. In the first place, I had thought it was a turnip she had in her hand and, secondly, it had seemed blasphemous to my eight-year-old ears, because *nobody* could have called on God as a witness in *our* house without a storm of disapproval. Over the years I have pondered the incongruity of such a hidebound preacher stepping right over the questionable methods Scarlett had to stoop to in her avoidance of hunger, to single out her determination. Was *he* so caught up in the honey of romance concerning the Lost Cause that the ends had come to justify the means for him? I suspect so.

Gone with the Wind illustrates another aspect of the romantic myth of the Confederacy that drew our willing participation. If there had been as many mansions in the South as people think there were, they would have had to be row houses. The one mansion in our neighborhood by that time had no veranda, was on the verge of falling down, and faced a levee some thirty yards from its front door. The other old houses still around that had been built before the Civil War, log or frame houses that never had been painted, were anything but grand. The fact is that the country was too new for antebellum grandeur. No matter, the mansions in our heads had been left in Virginia and Tennessee when the family came to Arkansas. People like mine, who probably had scratched out a marginal living for themselves and their slaves in those malaria-ridden swamps, had little in common with the characters at Tara except suffering and financial losses (on a smaller scale) brought by their participation in that idiotic, hopeless dream. And yet nostalgia for that Cause persisted. White southerners who claim not to be stirred by a band playing "Dixie" are probably lying; why else would there have been such fights in southern universities after integration, when the blacks put a stop to the song's being played at football games?

Although Jodie brought home a college friend from Wisconsin who charmed everybody in spite of his strange and horrible accent, "the North" to us was a terrible place where the chill in the weather was thought to be reflected in the people. But the truly unforgivable thing about the North was the social equality offered blacks. My lifelong ambition to attend the University of Chicago was thwarted by my father's flat refusal to allow me to attend classes with black people; he meant, of course, black *men*. And when I finally did go to Washington University in St. Louis, I had his cooperation because he did not think it was far enough north to allow integration. When I went, in 1952, he was almost right. There were very few black students at the university, and only one movie house in St. Louis, the Pageant, was integrated. Even so, differences were visible to me the minute I stepped off the train. On the taxi ride from the railroad station to the apartment my roommate had found for us, I saw the most shocking sight I had come upon by that point in my life: the sight, as I have already noted, was of blacks playing golf on the public links in Forest Park. That glimpse of normality marked the end of the first phase of my life, the phase I set out to clarify in these ruminations on the consequences of having been born in the Delta. For the simple sight of those black men playing golf, a sight that probably would not even have been noticed by somebody from the North, was, in my mind, like turning a corner and running into a burning bush. The sight called into question everything I had been led to believe up to that moment and constituted the first step in a long and painful journey toward revising my vision of the world – an odyssey that took considerably longer than Homer's, but which, like his, eventually led home. The world I left that day in 1952 had changed almost as much as I had by the time I returned in 1968 to take a job teaching at the University of Arkansas.

From 1952 to 1955, while I was in graduate school in St. Louis, I remember the impression of traveling backward in time when I went home. It was like getting on the train in the twentieth century and getting off in the vast flat Delta in the nineteenth. And again, the situation with black people was central to this perception. By that time, it was illegal to segregate trains that crossed state lines, so the train I took on the St. Louis–to–New Orleans run was integrated when we pulled out of the station in St. Louis at about seven in the evening. If you had a Pullman berth, you could ride undisturbed all the way to New Orleans, no matter what color you were. If you did not, it was necessary to get off the train in Little Rock at about midnight, walk up a flight of stairs, across the platform, down another flight of stairs, and reboard the same train. At that point a conductor segregated it. Sometimes there were separate cars for blacks and whites, sometimes the barrier was only a foot-high iron grille on the top of a pair of seats on both sides of the aisle. If the seats in the black section were all taken, blacks were expected to stand in the aisle down there instead of taking empty seats in the white part of the car. When I got on the train at Dumas for the return trip, I found the same situation; the train had been segregated in New Orleans. Blacks could not go to the club car below Little Rock and would not be seated at the same table with whites in the diner. The cooks, waiters, and porters were invariably black; conductors were white.

I do not mean to trivialize the black experience when I say that it was a situation demeaning to all. I felt debased – if not in the same degree, still debased – when a black passenger once kindly carried my bag across that platform for me, past the astonished conductor, who thought the bag was the man's own, into the "white" car and was heaving it onto the overhead rack before the conductor grabbed him by the collar and told him to get on back in the other car "where you belong." Nobody, including me, said anything to the conductor. I cannot to this day explain why I could not speak out, why my outrage could not find a voice, except for my moral inadequacy, which I have already mentioned. Even if all the other people in that crowded railroad car believed that the conductor was right, I did not. I knew better. So why did I not speak out? This was not a totalitarian regime. I was in the company of strangers a hundred miles from home and going further; no retribution could have fallen on my family or on me, except for the disapproval of those strangers on the train, which I would have had to endure for no more than the eight or so hours the journey took. All I can say is that my conditioning had been thorough. At twenty-two I did not have the courage to speak; I did not have the strength to march alone. While I was out of the South, even no further than St. Louis, it was possible to forget that things like this happened and that I was a participant, whether I wanted to be or not. Going north was an easy way out; racial matters seemed simple to my new northern friends, whose solutions ranged from a half-facetious scheme to slice the South off and float it away on the Gulf of Mexico to a serious plan for sending in the military for another occupation. Yet there were few, if any, black students at Washington University in those years, and, as I have already noted, I never saw them socially even in Minneapolis as late as 1968.

But still, the differences between southern and northern attitudes toward integration altered my vision so much that eventually it became almost impossible for me to go home for long visits. This alienation was reinforced by the insularity of my family and southern friends, who never could remember whether I lived in Minneapolis or Indianapolis, because, as far as they were concerned, it made no difference. Moreover, they were not enthusiastic about the change they felt in the air. Those who always had seemed most liberal began to backtrack when social justice meant sending their children to integrated schools. So, after my father's death in 1957, my ties with the Delta wore thin, although I was called upon to "explain" the phenomenon of the integration crisis at Central High School in Little Rock by everyone I met who heard that I was from Arkansas. It is usually the only thing foreigners have ever heard about Little Rock. In the sixteen years I was away, I lived in Missouri, Minnesota, England, and Denmark, and I traveled to many other places. I went through the graduate programs at two different universities and inevitably changed and grew. But, as I said in the beginning, the Delta was always in my head. And because it was changing, too, I could finally come back to live within three hundred miles of it.

This became possible because, during the years I was away, the South entered the twentieth century. In a short span of time, the civil rights laws of 1964 and 1965 and the enforcement of the Supreme Court ruling on integration of the schools made differences in the condition of black people that are almost unbelievable. Although there is little social integration even now (eleven o'clock on Sunday morning is still probably the most segregated hour in the South), the change in the situation of black people is real and profound. If we are not yet where we should be, at least we are on the way. I left the South because I felt powerless to do anything about a situation that I found unbearable. I returned feeling that it was time to put my shoulder to a wheel now free to turn. I might well be asked how I think my presence can make a difference, and it may be illusion on

my part to think it can. However, as a professor of English in the state
university, I am in a position requiring the discussion of values with
students who are going to be the leaders of this society. I can only
hope that my teaching has the same effect on some of my students
that my high school English teacher's had on me. It may be a drop
in the bucket, but it's my drop and, as I finally came to understand,
my bucket.